D1483034

JOHN PAUL II
AND HIS
CARDINALS

JOHN PAUL II AND HIS CARDINALS

GRZEGORZ GAŁĄZKA

Text by
MARIA MORETTI

MIDWEST THEOLOGICAL FORUM   **URBI ET ORBI COMMUNICATIONS**

Project Director and Photographer
Grzegorz Gałązka

Preface
Giuseppe De Carli

Text
Maria Moretti

Layout
Giuseppe Sabatelli

Editorial supervision
Nicolò Suffi

Editorial Supervision, English Edition
Robert Moynihan

Translation
Tariq Hager and Shena Muldoon

Film preparation / Pre-press
Scanner Europa

Publisher
Libreria Editrice Vaticana
00120 Città del Vaticano

Co-Publishers:
In Polish: *Michalineum*
In French: *Éditions du Signe*
In English: *Midwest Theological Forum*
            Urbi et Orbi Communications
ISBN
1-890177-13-X

2001 © Copyright photographs Grzegorz Gałązka
All rights reserved.
No part of this publication may be reproduced without written permission.

Addresses and Contact numbers

URBI ET ORBI COMMUNICATIONS

Rome: *Inside the Vatican*
Via delle Mura Aurelie 7c
00165 Rome, Italy
Tel: 0039 (06) 3938-7471
E-mail: itvrome@tuttopmi.it

USA: c/o St. Martin de Porres Printshop
3050 Gap Knob Road
New Hope, KY 40052
Tel: 1-800-789-9494
Web Site: insidethevatican.com

MIDWEST THEOLOGICAL FORUM

712 S. Loomis St.
Chicago, IL 60607 USA
Tel: (312) 421-8135
Fax: (312) 421-8129
E-mail: rodegaard@attglobal.net

15

Preface

by Giuseppe De Carli

"For 16 years I was unable to celebrate Mass. Except once, when I was being transferred from one prison camp to another. A guard gave me a bit of bread and some wine. I consecrated the bread and wine with my handcuffs still on my wrists and with chains around my ankles."

The old man spoke slowly, remembering. His hair unkempt, his expression intense but friendly, Alexandru Todea, cardinal of Holy Mother Church, oriental rite bishop of Alba Iulia and Catholic Primate of Romania, recalled the times of persecution. It was 1991, and the Iron Curtain had just fallen.

"In prison they taught us two things: that the greatest enemy of mankind was the Pope, and that whoever wanted to be a good Romanian should become Orthodox," he said.

Three years of solitary confinement. Todea could have become bitter, vengeful. But he chose another way.

"I never doubted my faith," His Eminence said. "I never compromised my conscience. Now," he added, "we have decided to pardon everyone, including those who persecuted us. We don't want to see them punished."

This Primate, this "Prince" of the Church, was able not only to shake free from slavery's chains, but also to share the bread of forgiveness.

Todea was nearly 80. During our talk, at certain moments, he trembled.

As a young man, he had been sent to Rome to study at the college of Propaganda Fide. One day in St. Peter's Basilica, he decided to make a promise before God: "Lord, if I do not remain faithful to this course that I have embarked upon for my entire life, I prefer to die."

And as he spoke, the indomitable cardinal broke down and wept uncontrollably before the television cameras.

I recall those tears with perfect clarity. The first cardinal to break into tears on live television. I have the tape of that interview, and I conserve it like a relic, because it bears witness to the greatness of a man at the moment of his abandonment, with all defenses down.

If he could go back and change anything, I asked him, would he have lived his life differently? The question was a little bit silly.

Todea looked at me, gathered himself immediately, and replied proudly, in his halting Italian: "If I were forced to choose between prison and being a cardinal, I wouldn't hesitate. I would still choose the first."

As I covered the first Consistory of the new millennium (February 21-22, 2001) for Italian television, I connected other names with that of Todea: Tomašek, Beran, Wyszyński, Stepinac, Koliqi, Korec, Kung Pin-Mei, Vlk, Kozłowiecki, Świątek, Nguyên Van Thuân, Ocampo Posadas (the third cardinal assassinated during the 20th century). All cardinals who suffered persecution. For them, the Pope's words — *"Accipite biretum rubrum, cardinalatus dignitatis insigne, per quod significatur usque ad sanguinis effusionem..."* ("Receive the red hat, sign of cardinalatial dignity, by which is signified witness even unto the shedding of blood") — were their personal history. And John Paul II explained what this meant: "Uncompromising fidelity, fidelity even unto the ultimate sacrifice."

I was moved by the splendor and drama of the ritual. The color red and the exaltation of individuals within the community of the Church created a stark spiritual contrast. On the one hand, ecclesial grandeur; on the other, "the cross, throne of God in the world," as Pope Wojtyła put it with eloquence and power. Certainly I was reminded of the Renaissance, of the age when cardinals were patrons of the arts, ruled palaces and courts, moved with pomp and in rich robes, wore the wide-brimmed "galero" hat and great sweeping capes. Of all that, only a remnant has remained: a simple robe, the *mozzetta* (an elbow-length cape) and, on solemn occasions, a robe inlaid with red silk.

Grzegorz Gałązka investigates even this post-conciliar cardinalatial "uniform," carrying his camera into the tailor's shop. And he does it, as always, with modesty, respectfully, but with an habitual and persuasive assurance. Those cardinals who look at themselves, with a smile of self-deprecating irony, in the mirror give us a glimpse into an unexpected and little-known human dimension — a glimpse into the smile of the Church.

Leafing through these portraits, one gets a sense of the distance between reality and the journalistic analyses ("this one could be the next Pope, this one no...") which have tormented the first months of the new millennium — the model of analysis many observers and commentators on religious affairs, perhaps against their will, have embraced in recent years.

And so there are two contrasting viewpoints: the *"disciplina arcani"* ("the contemplation of hidden things") and the rumble of the media – the floodlights of a global film set and... the silence of mystery. To use the words of Pope Wojtyła: "The mystical barque of the Church is preparing for the open sea. *Duc in altum!* (Luke 5:4) Put out into the deep!"

Cardinal John Henry Newman, called by Pius XII *"acerrimus veritatis investigator"* ("most relentless seeker after truth") spoke of this reality in fresh and clear terms. As he accepted the purple from Pope Pius IX, he wrote: "The Church should do nothing other than continue in her task, in trust and in peace; she must remain firm and serene and await God's salvation." Then he cited Psalm 36: "The meek shall inherit the earth."

WHO ARE THE CARDINALS?

by Maria Moretti

On January 20, 2001, John Paul II announced the creation of 37 new cardinals. On January 28, he disclosed the identity of two cardinals nominated *in pectore* at the Consistory of 1998 and made public the names of another five members of the College of Cardinals. These are the first new cardinals of the new millennium.

During the Consistory of February 21, 2001, John Paul II described the essential characteristics of cardinals with the following words: "The Son of Man also came not to be served but to serve, and to give his life as a ransom for many' (*Mk* 10:45). The Evangelist Mark's words help us to understand better the profound meaning of an event like the Consistory we are celebrating. The Church does not rely on human calculations and powers, but on Jesus Christ crucified and on the consistent witness born to him by the apostles, martyrs and confessors of the faith. This witness can also demand the heroism of total self-giving to God and to others. Every Christian knows that he is called to an uncompromising fidelity, which may even require the ultimate sacrifice. And you in particular, venerable Brothers, raised to the dignity of Cardinal, know this. You are committed to faithfully following Christ, the Martyr *par excellence* and the faithful Witness.

"Your service to the Church is also expressed in assisting and collaborating with the Successor of Peter, in order to lighten the burden of a ministry that extends to the ends of the earth. Together with him, you must be strenuous defenders of the truth and guardians of the heritage of faith and morals which originated in the Gospel. You will thus be reliable guides for everyone and, in the first place, for priests, consecrated persons and committed lay people.

"The Pope counts on your help in serving the Christian community, which is confidently entering the third millennium. As true Pastors, you will know how to be alert sentinels defending the flock entrusted to you by the 'Chief Shepherd,' who is preparing for you 'the unfading crown of glory' (1 *Pt* 5:4).

"Beginning today a very special bond links you with Peter's Successor, who by Christ's will — as has been rightly recalled — is 'the perpetual and visible source and foundation of the unity both of the Bishops and of the whole company of the faithful' (*Lumen gentium*, n. 23). This link makes you, in a new way, eloquent signs of communion. If you promote communion, the entire Church will benefit. St Peter Damian, whose liturgical memorial occurs today, says: 'It is unity that makes the many parts into a single whole, which brings different human wills together in a framework of love and harmony of spirit' (*Opusc*. XIII, 24).

"The 'many parts' of the Church are expressed in you, whose experiences have matured on various continents and in various services to the People of God. It is essential that the 'parts' you represent should be gathered into 'a single whole' through love, which is the bond of perfection. Only in this way will Christ's prayer be fulfilled: 'that they may all be one; even as you, Father, are in me, and I in you, that they also may be in us, so that the world may believe that you have sent me' (cf. *Jn* 7:21).

"From the Second Vatican Council to this day, much has been done to enlarge the areas of individual responsibility in the service of ecclesial communion. There is no doubt that with God's grace it will be possible to do even more. Today you are proclaimed and created Cardinals so that you will dedicate yourselves, to the extent of your responsibility, to increasing the spirituality of communion in the Church. For it alone, 'by prompting a trust and openness wholly in accord with the dignity and responsibility of every member of the People of God, supplies institutional reality with a soul' (*Novo millennio ineunte*, n. 45).

"Venerable Brothers, you are the first Cardinals to be created in the new millennium. After having drawn in abundance from the sources of divine mercy during the Holy Year, the mystical barque of the Church is preparing anew 'to put out into the deep,' to bring the message of salvation to the world. Together let us unfurl her sails to the wind of the Spirit, examining the signs of the times and interpreting them in the light of the Gospel, to answer 'the ever-recurring questions which men ask about the meaning of this present life and of the life to come' (*Gaudium et spes*, n. 4).

"The world is becoming ever more complex and changeable, and the acute awareness of the existing discrepancies creates or increases contradictions and imbalances (cf. *ibid.*, n. 8). The enormous potential of scientific and technological progress, as well as the phenomenon of globalization that is extending to ever new areas, require us to be open to dialogue with every person and every social institution, with the intention of giving to each an account for the hope that is in us (cf. *1 Pt* 3:15).

"However, venerable Brothers, we know that to face these new tasks effectively, it is necessary to foster an ever deeper communion with the Lord. It is precisely the red colour of the robes you wear that reminds you of this urgent need. Is that colour not the symbol of ardent love for Christ? Does that bright red not symbolize the burning fire of love for the Church which must nurture within you the readiness, if necessary, to bear the supreme witness of bloodshed? '*Usque ad effusionem sanguinis*,' says the ancient formula. In looking at you, the People of God must be able to find a concrete and shining reference-point that will spur them to be truly the light of the world and the salt of the earth (cf. *Mt* 5:13).

"You come from 27 countries on four continents and speak various languages. Is this not a sign of the Church's ability, now that she has spread to every corner of the globe, to understand peoples with different traditions and languages, in order to bring to all the message of Christ? In him and only in him can we find salvation. This is the truth that today we would like to reaffirm together. Christ walks with us and guides our steps."

In his homily the following day, February 22, John Paul II firmly stressed, "Do not doubt that as it was for Christ and Peter thus it will also be for you: your most efficacious testimony will always be that signaled by the Cross. *The Cross is the throne of God in the world.* Upon the cross, Christ offered humanity its most important lesson: to love one another as he loved us (cf. *Jn* 13:34) — even to the extreme of sacrificing oneself."

CARDINAL MARTYRS

The willingness to serve the Church to the extreme sacrifice of one's own life is demonstrated in the lives of many cardinals who suffered even to the point of martyrdom in the course of history. Here we name only a few. Five years in the concentration camps of Auschwitz and Dachau and 50 years of missionary life in Africa failed to convince Adam Kozlowiecki, an 87-year-old Pole, to leave the jungles of Zambia to reside in Rome after he was created cardinal in 1998 by John Paul II. Frantisek Tomasek of Prague, "the old oak-tree of the Spirit," was arrested and interned in the work camp of Zeliv in 1951. Pope Paul VI named him a cardinal *in pectore* in 1976. Tomasek fought indefatigably to the venerable age of 92 for religious freedom and the independence of the Church in his country,

Czechoslovakia. His successor is Miloslav Vlk, cardinal since November 26, 1994. From a humble background, Vlk pursued his vocation while at the same time working in a factory, on farms and as a window-washer. Thinking "Christ also felt abandoned, but continued to carry his cross to the ultimate triumph of the resurrection," Vlk patiently waited, without hatred or bitterness, for the end of the long period of Communist persecution of the Church in Czechoslovakia.

Ocampo Posadas of Mexico spoke out against the social malaise breeding violence and criminality in his country. Soon after, on May 24, 1993, he was assassinated, making him the third cardinal killed in the last century. Victim of the Albanian Communist regime, Mikel Koliqi spent 44 years in prison (21 years of hard labor and 23 of confinement) before being freed in 1986. He was created cardinal at the age of 92 by John Paul II on November 26, 1994. Belarussian Kazimierz Świątek lived a personal calvary from 1941 to 1954 — arrested, repeatedly imprisoned and condemned to forced labor for 10 years. The life of Slovak cardinal Ján Chryzostom Korec was also a continuous struggle from 1948 to 1990 due to the Communist regime. Consecrated clandestinely, arrested and condemned to 12 years of prison, Korec was freed in 1968 and received by Paul VI in 1969. He was then forced to spend another 20 dark years, unable to celebrate Mass or publish books. John Paul II made him a cardinal at the consistory of 1991.

THE CHURCH — THE PEOPLE OF GOD,
THE BISHOP OF ROME, THE EPISCOPAL
AND CARDINALATIAL COLLEGES

"The Church presents herself as a people assembled by the unity of the Father and the Son and the Holy Spirit" (*Lumen Gentium* 4). Jesus, after his ascension into heaven, sent forth his apostles, just as he had been sent forth by His Father. The apostles founded Christian communities in all parts of the world. The heads of the local churches, subsequently called bishops, selected their collaborators and consecrated priests and deacons. Deacons, priest-presbyters and bishops were called to exercise their ministry for the people of God through the sacrament of Holy Orders. The successors of St. Peter, head of the apostles and first Bishop of Rome, serve as guides for the universal Church.

Later, bishops were chosen by the clergy and the people of a city, as in the case of St. Ambrose, governor and then Bishop of Milan.

After the fall of the Roman Empire, kings and emperors intervened in the elections of bishops and sometimes even took over the episcopal residences. In the 11th century, Pope Gregory VII, Bishop of Rome, after the bitter Investiture Controversy with the emperor, won independence for the Church and established that bishops can be elected only by the clergy. In every diocese, the people who most closely worked with the bishops were considered "*persone cardinali*" ("cardinal" or "hinge" persons) for they functioned as "hinges" between the bishop and the people of God. The Latin word "*cardo, cardinis*" means, in fact, "hinge." The Bishop of Rome was elected by the presbyters and "cardinal" deacons.

The word "cardinal" soon changed from an adjective into a noun. Three ranks of cardinals emerged — cardinal bishops, cardinal priests and cardinal deacons. In 1059, Pope Nicholas II established that the Bishop of Rome could be elected only by the cardinal bishops.

Due to the growing administrative burdens of the Church, the cardinals from the three orders were constrained to leave their sees and remain in the Roman Curia. But they kept their ancient titles, even though their episcopal residences, titles and functions were administered by others.

Pope Leo IX broke new ground, granting the title of cardinal to people also living outside of Rome — above all to those embracing the Gregorian reforms initiated by Gregory VII. By the 13th century, even non-Italians could be created cardinals and the College of Cardinals became increasingly numerous.

In 1962, John XXIII extended episcopal consecration to the entire College of Cardinals. Thus, all cardinals are now, in principle, bishops. An exception exists only for those upon whom the title of cardinal is conferred due to distinguished merit in the theological field.

In the Magisterium and in the pastoral government of the Church, the Episcopal College and the Roman pontiff, its head as Bishop of Rome, pursued the work of the apostles. At first, the pontiff depended on various priests and deacons whom he sent as emissaries and papal legates. In more important cases, the Pope summoned synods and councils. Over time, the expansion of the Church forced the Pope to rely increasingly on the counsel of the cardinals, who soon became his principle collaborators.

THE SELECTION OF CARDINALS

The Supreme Pontiff chooses his cardinals in complete independence from civil authority. His candidates are drawn from among male faithful who are at least in the order of priesthood and who distinguish themselves by their morals, their piety, their knowledge and their competence, whatever their nationality. In theory, a lay person can also be created cardinal, since from the theological point of view, the Cardinalate is not of divine origin. However, canon law is firmly committed to a College of Cardinals strictly tied to the clergy.

At the beginning of the second millennium, the number of cardinals was limited to 24. In 1586, Pope Sixtus V fixed the number of cardinals at 70 and divided the Cardinalate into the three orders which exist to this day — 6 cardinal bishops, to whom are entrusted the suburbicarian dioceses; 50 cardinal priests, each of whom is given the title of a church in Rome; and 14 cardinal deacons assigned to diaconate churches in Rome. The suburbicarian dioceses are Porto and Santa Rufina, Albano, Palestrina, Frascati, Sabina and Poggio Mieteto, Velletri and Ostia. Ostia, the seventh suburbicarian diocese, is assigned to the Dean of the College of Cardinals.

In 1958, John XXIII raised the number of cardinals to 75. In 1965, Paul VI already had 144 cardinals available to him, inserting into the College eastern Patriarchs, who were the bishops of their Patriarchal sees.

The internationalization of the College of Cardinals has benefited both the entire Church and the represented nations. From a clear predominance of Italians in the 12th century, in 2001, out of 183 cardinals, only 41 are Italian. From the beginning of the College of Cardinals to today, more than 3,000 cardinals have been created. Of this number, 201 have been made by John Paul II.

FORMALITIES — THE PRESENT AND THE PAST

All newly-chosen cardinals receive a booklet *Vestes S.R.E. Cardinalium*, in Italian and Latin, describing the appropriate dress to wear on specific occasions. Two basic categories of dress constitute cardinal attire — "choral" and "simple."

Choral attire includes a cassock of red cotton with hemming, lacing, and buttons of red silk and a *mozzetta* (elbow-length cape) of the same material. The cassock is hoodless, with a flush-red silken sash, fringed at both ends. Other accessories include deep-red socks, collar, *zucchetto* (skull-cap), red silk *biretta*, a rochet made of linen or similar material, a pectoral cross with a red-gold cord, and a ring. The ring is a "symbol of dignity, of pastoral care, and of the most profound communion with the See of Peter."

The simple dress is a cassock without oversleeves. It has hemming, lacing, button holes and buttons of red silk. It can be worn with a pelerine, a cloak decorated in a way similar to the cassock. If it is used regularly, it can be undecorated. Black socks have to be worn with a black cassock; they can be red if wearing a decorated cassock. The cape is black. The black velvet hat can be adorned with red-yellow chords and ribbons. A pectoral cross with a chain and a ring complete the "simple" attire.

A progressive reduction in dress formality has occurred since 1870. The traditional *galero*, a big red hat, and shoes with buckles and other ornaments, are now items of the past. The white cape with 70 ermine hides, a symbol of purity, has also disappeared. The *cappa magna*, a cloak with a train made from 24 meters of silk, historically used to cover the back parts of a horse, has been reduced to a simple red cloth. The red mantlet, sash with buckles, the red cloak or cape, and the red velvet hat have been abolished. The typical cardinal garment is only the purple (*porpora*), from which comes the synonym for cardinals, "*Porporati*" ("enpurpled"). Only in the most solemn of circumstances and outside of Rome can the *cappa magna* be worn — without the ermine.

During Consistory ceremonies — the ceremonies at

which cardinals are created — the newly-elected cardinals have to appear with a cassock of red cloth and a red-fringed sash, collar, red socks, *mozzetta*, rochet, black shoes, pectoral cross with a silken red-and-gold cord and a bishop's ring. The *biretta* has three segments and is worn with the missing part on the left. The secretaries of the cardinals wear a cassock decorated with a purple band or if black with a black band, depending on whether they are prelates or chaplains of His Holiness. The same rules apply for the concelebration and the giving of the ring. Cardinals do not have to wear the ring but have to possess the *biretta*, the skull-cap and the white mitre.

Furthermore, each cardinal must have an emblem (coat-of-arms) with the cardinal's motto and the picture of a red hat with its two lateral cords hanging with 30 tassels of the same color, 15 on each side, displayed in five successive rows of 1, 2, 3, 4 and 5. The staff and mitre are no longer necessary. Cardinals of episcopal, archepiscopal or patriarchal rank have the single or double shield and trefoil cross, depending on their rank. In a *sede vacante* period (when the papal see is vacant), the cardinal chamberlain of Holy Roman Church places the pontifical standard with its two keys, one gold and one silver, above his hat. The cardinal's arms can be displayed outside his titular church, along with his name near the main door; oil portraits of the cardinals, once common, are now rare.

THE CONFERRING OF THE TITLE

The Roman Pontiff confers the title of cardinal through a decree made public before the College of Cardinals. The Ordinary Consistory of February 21, 2001 in St. Peter's Square followed the rite introduced at the June 21, 1991 Consistory, using the Liturgy of the Word. After the liturgical greeting, the Pope solemnly proclaimed the names of the new cardinals. Cardinal Giovanni Battista Re, the first named, on behalf of all, delivered an address of praise and gratitude.

After the Liturgy of the Word, the homily of the Holy Father, and the profession of faith, the new cardinals swore their fidelity and obedience to the Holy Father and his successors. In accordance with the order of creation, each cardinal knelt in front of John Paul II to receive the scarlet cardinal *biretta*. The Pope then assigned each of the new cardinals a church in Rome, as a sign of the cardinals' assistance to the Pope in the religious life of the city. The Pope then handed to each cardinal the Papal Bull of creation and gave him the sign of peace, which he in turn gave to all the other cardinals. The prayer of the faithful, the recital of the Our Father, and a final benediction closed the celebration. In the late afternoon of the same day, the new cardinals received courtesy calls in the Apostolic Palace and the Paul VI Audience Hall.

On February 22, on the occasion of the Feast of The Chair of St. Peter at the Basilica, John Paul II presided over the celebration of the Eucharist with the new cardinals and gave them their rings. During the course of the homily, he affirmed: "Today's celebration highlights *the role of Peter and his successors* in steering the boat of the Church across this 'ocean.' It is therefore especially significant that at this liturgical celebration, the College of Cardinals should be beside the Pope, including the new cardinals created yesterday at the first Consistory after the Great Jubilee."

The Pope then added: "How can we forget that the Petrine ministry, the visible principle of unity, constitutes a difficulty for the other Churches and Ecclesial Communities? (cf. Encyclical *Ut unum sint*, n. 88). But at the same time, how can we not recall the historical fact that in the first millennium the primatial role of the Bishop of Rome was exercised without encountering any resistance in the Church of either the West or the East? Today I would like in a special way to pray to the Lord with you that the new millennium we have entered may soon see this situation overcome and full communion re-established. May the Holy Spirit give all believers the necessary light and strength to achieve what the Lord so ardently desires. I ask you to help me and to collaborate in every way in this demanding mission.

"Venerable Brother Cardinals, the ring that you wear and which I will shortly present to the new members of the College highlights the special bond that joins you to this Apostolic See."

The pontiff can choose to keep the names of some of his chosen cardinals secret — they then become so-called "cardinals *in pectore*." Cardinals are secretly nominated when, for political or other reasons, they would be personally endangered or their ministry would be hampered by having their elevation publicly revealed. From the moment their promotions are made public, the newly elected *in pectore* assume the official duties and privileges of their office.

The creation *in pectore* is nullified in the event of a sudden death of the Pontiff. John Paul II has created a total of three cardinals *in pectore* in the course of his pontificate. The choice of Ignatius Kung Pin-Mei was made at the Consistory of June 30, 1979 and rendered public at the Consistory of June 28, 1991. Marian Jaworski, Archbishop of Leopoli for the Catholics of the Latin rite and Janis Pujats, Archbishop of Riga, Lithuania, chosen in 1998, were made public in 2001.

On February 23, 2001, at an audience for the new cardinals, John Paul II said: "I address my cordial greetings to you, dear Ukrainian pilgrims, on this solemn day on which two sons of your country have been created cardinals together — one from the Latin rite, and the other from the Eastern rite. Pray that this sign of unity becomes a token of full communion between the West and the East."

PRINCIPAL RIGHTS, DUTIES AND FUNCTIONS

Cardinals remain such from their creation to their natural death. "Eminence" is the honorific given them since 1630. They are also known as "Princes of the

Church."

Cardinals benefit from various privileges under the Italian legal code. At public ceremonies, they follow the President of the Republic on the list of honorable precedence. They can testify in a place of their choosing, in their house or office. Their liturgical privileges consist of broad powers in relation to confession, the granting of indulgences, confirmation and minor orders. The *privilegium canonis* and the *privilegium fori* establish that only the Holy Father can judge cardinals and remove them from office.

The cardinals living in Rome carry on an active and continued cooperation with the central government of the Church. Some of them head the various ministries, or "dicasteries," of the Roman Curia and other important organs of the Holy See, and are then called "cardinals of the Curia." The Curial cardinals formerly received a salary called the "cardinal plate" and the "cardinal roll." The cardinal plate (also called the "*distribuzione di capello*," literally "distribution of hat") was an annual pension given by the Pope if the cardinal's other revenue proved insufficient, paid monthly by the Administration of the Patrimony of the Apostolic See. The "cardinal roll" was a sum of money taken from the income of the Sacred College, and was also given to non-resident cardinals if they were in Rome on temporary duty (the amount was proportional to the length of the stay).

The increasing administrative complexity of the universal Church led to the creation of the Congregations. The cardinal heads of the Congregations or other ministries of the Roman Curia and the presiding cardinal of the Supreme Court of the Apostolic Signature have the title of Prefect. Cardinals can also be Presidents of other curial and para-curial bodies (Pontifical Councils, Commissions and Offices). The cardinal prefects and presidents customarily resign from office when they turn 75.

The residential cardinal bishops reside in their respective dioceses. They are also members of the Roman Congregations and are invited to participate at the Consistories and at the plenary reunions.

The Holy Father is also aided by the Secretariat of State, presided over by a Cardinal Secretary of State and divided into two departments: the Department of General Affairs of the Church and the Department of State Relations. The Cardinal Secretary of State administers the Holy See's property and the finances transferred to the Roman Curia through the Administration of the Patrimony of the Apostolic See.

The Pope has his official residence in the Basilica of St. John Lateran, the cathedral of the Bishop of Rome, and delegates the government of the Diocese of Rome to the Cardinal Vicar, presently Cardinal Camillo Ruini. In the event of a vacant see and a contemporaneous vacancy in the Vicariate of Rome, the Vice-regent exercises ordinary jurisdiction and performs the functions of the Cardinal Vicar, which do not end with the death of the Pope. In the event of a vacant see, the Sacred College must be informed of the actions of the Vicar of Rome. The Pope's Vicar General for the Vatican and for the Pontifical Villa of Castel Gandolfo is, instead, the Cardinal Archpriest *pro tempore* of St. Peter's Basilica.

COLLEGIALITY, UNITY AND COMMUNION
AMONG THE PRINCES OF THE CHURCH

Collegiality is a priority both in the governance of the State of Vatican City and in the governance of the universal Church.

The Supreme Pontiff is in charge of the Vatican City government, according to a new law in effect since February 22, 2001. John Paul II modified the preceding law of June 7, 1929, aware "of the necessity to give a systematic and organic form to the changes introduced in successive phases in the juridical system of the state of Vatican City." He wished to provide a "guarantee of the freedom of the Apostolic See and assure the real and visible independence of the Roman Pontiff in the exercise of his mission in the world." The Pope is an absolute sovereign with the complete powers of a monarch elected for life. However, he entrusts the exercise of legislative power, with some specific exceptions, to a Commission of Cardinals, nominated by himself, who have 5-year terms. He delegates executive power to the President of the Commission. Civil powers — legislative, executive and juridical — are left to the Supreme Pontiff, as the Sovereign of the Vatican City State. During a vacant see, these powers pass to the College of Cardinals. Legislative power, however, has to be exercised with great discretion, solely in cases of emergency, and is effective solely for the period of the vacancy, unless confirmed by the new pontiff.

The College of Cardinals is endowed with juridical powers in the Church government and is represented and presided over by the oldest cardinal bishop, the Cardinal Dean, presently Cardinal Bernardin Gantin, as the *primus inter pares* (first among equals). In the event of physical impediment, this role is assumed by the Vice-Dean, the Bishop of Porto and Santa Rufina — presently Cardinal Joseph Ratzinger. If the office of the Dean or of the Vice-Dean becomes vacant, the cardinals assigned to the suburbicarian titular churches elect a substitute. The Dean and Vice-Dean have to live in Rome. At a Secret Consistory, the Pope temporarily nominates the Chamberlain of the Sacred College, currently Cardinal Eduardo Martinez Somalo, from among the cardinals living in Rome. The Chamberlain has the task of administering the Church's property. The Secretary of the Congregation for Bishops, accompanied by a vice-secretary and a treasurer, assumes the function of Secretary of the College of the Cardinals.

The solemn gathering in Rome of all the cardinals, presided over by the Supreme Pontiff, takes the name of Consistory ("where [the cardinals] find themselves together"). Consistories are not held according to a pre-established calendar. If the purpose of the reunion is to discuss serious questions or acts of the greatest solemnity, an Ordinary Consistory is convened. Otherwise, particular needs of the Church or questions of exceptional importance require the convocation of an Extraordinary Consistory. The Ordinary Consistory, Private or Secret, takes place at the Consistory Hall in the Apostolic Palace. The Public or Solemn Extraordinary Consistory is held in the Paul VI Audience Hall. The Pope and all cardinals present in Rome participate at the Ordinary Consistory for the creation and making public of the new cardinals and for the nomination of the Chamberlain. These Consistories are also where Cardinal Deacons receive priestly sees, where new episcopal appointments are announced, and where canonizations proposed by the Congregation for the Causes of Saints are examined. On occasions of particular solemnity, the Consistories can be public involving the participation of members of the private Consistory, prelates, delegates from civil society and other invitees.

The Consistory of February 21, 2001 was an Ordinary Public Consistory. John Paul II convened an Extraordinary Consistory in 1994 to discuss a Church *mea culpa* for sins committed by Church members throughout the centuries. On March 12, 2000, John Paul II solemnly pronounced an act of penitence. He reiterated the *mea culpa* in a prayer while on a visit to Jerusalem, referring in particular to the horrors of anti-Semitism. In May 2001, the convocation of another Extraordinary Consistory reunited all the cardinals in Rome to discuss the theme of unity and collaboration in the Church in view of a new global evangelization effort and an intensification of relations with other Christian churches, with special attention to the assistance the cardinals and bishops can offer the Pope in governing the Church.

During periods in which the Apostolic See is vacant, the College of Cardinals temporarily carries out extraordinary functions, as outlined by John Paul II's Constitution of February 23, 1996 *Universi Dominici Gregis*: *Concerning the Vacancy of the Apostolic See and the Election of the Roman Pontiff*. The reason for amending this Constitution was to take note of the great changes the Church is living through and of the renewal of canon law through the Code of Canon Law of 1983 and the Code of Canons of the Eastern Churches of 1990. Nevertheless, radical departures from pre-existing Church norms and structures did not occur — rather document recognizes the validity of the "wise and venerable tradition in effect up to now."

A vacancy in the Apostolic See occurs in the event of the death or loss of reason of the Holy Father or if the pontifical dignity is freely renounced, from the moment one of those conditions is recognized until the election of a new pontiff. During the period of vacancy, the government of the Church is entrusted to the College of Cardinals. The Cardinals have limited powers, restricted to carrying out the ordinary and necessary functions essential to the management of the Church — and to electing the new Pope. The general Congregations,

assemblies of all the cardinals in the Apostolic Palace, presided over by the Dean or, if not possible, then by the Vice Dean, deliberate the most urgent and important questions. Issues of a lesser or routine nature are discussed at the particular Congregations composed of the Cardinal Chamberlain and three other cardinals, called Assistants, one from each order, chosen randomly from among the electors present in Rome and renominated every three days. At the general and particular Congregations, cardinals have to wear a black gown decorated with a red sash, *zucchetto*, pectoral cross and ring. Daily preparatory general congregations precede the beginning of the real election; these start from the day fixed by the Chamberlain and include the senior cardinal from each order. The cardinals' offices cease with the death of the Pope. An exception is made for the Major Penitentiary and the Chamberlain of Holy Mother Church. Congregations and apostolic tribunals continue to function, as far as ordinary activities are concerned. Should the office of Chamberlain be vacant at the death of the Holy Father, Chamberlain functions are exercised by the cardinal dean who unites the College to nominate a replacement until the election of the new Pope.

The Cardinal Chamberlain has to perform a series of duties proscribed by the above-mentioned Constitution. Among these, he has to oversee the administration of the property and temporal rights of the vacant see, taking immediate possession of the Vatican Apostolic Palace, the Lateran Palace and the Villa of Castel Gandolfo. The Chamberlain has the duty to ask for reports on the patrimonial and economic status of the various administrations and on the operations of an extraordinary nature currently underway.

The Prefecture of the Economic Affairs of the Holy See has to furnish the Chamberlain a general and projected budget. The data gathered are examined by the College of Cardinals. During the vacancy of the Apostolic See, the Cardinal Dean convokes the cardinals for congregations, for the the Conclave, and directs the electoral operations. If the Dean is 80 years old, he is substituted by the Vice Dean, or if the latter is also 80 years of age or over, by the oldest cardinal, who follows according to the general order of precedence.

THE ELECTION OF THE POPE

According to John Paul II: "While it is indeed a doctrine of faith that the power of the Supreme Pontiff derives directly from Christ, whose earthly Vicar he is, it is also certain that the supreme power in the Church is granted to him 'through a lawful election, accepted by him, together with episcopal consecration.'"

"The body to which is given the office of overseeing the election of the Roman Pontiff" is the College of Cardinals of the Holy Roman Church. Confirming what was envisioned by Paul VI in the Motu Proprio *Ingravescentem aetatem* of November 21, 1970, John Paul II stressed that the active electorate can be represented solely by cardinals under 80 years old from the day of the beginning of the vacant See and cannot exceed 120 members.

The College of Cardinals represents two essential characteristics of the papal office: its Roman and its universal nature. Referring to the cardinal electors, John Paul II stated: "In them one finds expressed in a remarkable synthesis the two aspects which characterize the figure and office of the Roman Pontiff: *Roman,* because identified with the Bishop of the Church in Rome and thus closely linked to the clergy of this City, represented by the Cardinals of the presbyteral and diaconal titles of Rome, and to the Cardinal Bishops of the suburbicarian Sees; *Pontiff of the universal Church,* because called to represent visibly the unseen Pastor who leads his whole flock to the pastures of eternal life. The universality of the Church is clearly expressed in the very composition of the College of Cardinals, whose members come from every continent.

"In the present historical circumstances, the universality of the Church seems sufficiently expressed by the College of 120 electors, made up of Cardinals coming from all parts of the world and from very different cultures. I therefore confirm that this is to be the maximum number of Cardinal electors, while at the same time indicating that it is in no way meant as a sign of less respect that the provision laid down by my predecessor Pope Paul VI has been retained, namely, that those Cardinals who celebrate their 80th birthday before the day when the Apostolic See becomes vacant do not take part in the election.

"The reason for this provision is the desire not to add to the weight of such venerable age the further burden of responsibility for choosing the one who will have to lead Christ's flock in ways adapted to the needs of the times. This does not however mean that the Cardinals over 80 years of age cannot take part in the preparatory meetings of the Conclave, in conformity with the norms set forth below. During the vacancy of the Apostolic See, and especially during the election of the Supreme Pontiff, they in particular should lead the People of God assembled in the Patriarchal Basilicas of Rome and in other churches in the Dioceses throughout the world, supporting the work of the electors with fervent prayers and supplications to the Holy Spirit and imploring for them the light needed to make their choice before God alone and with concern only for the 'salvation of souls, which in the Church must always be the supreme law.'"

Thus, as the Pope is the Bishop of Rome and earthly Vicar of the unseen Pastor of the universal flock, likewise the cardinals represent the clergy of Rome. Because they come from every continent, they also represent the universality of the Church. John Paul II, though keeping Paul VI's rule, has set one of its norms aside — today there are 134 cardinal electors, 14 more than the established limit. The assembly of the electors of the Pope, the restricted place where the assembly is held and the procedures followed for the election are referred to as the Conclave, a word derived from "*cum clave*" or "with a key."

The institution of the Conclave dates back to the work of Gregory X with the 1274 Constitution *Urbi periculum.* The document was drafted to chart a means of avoiding lengthy vacancies of the Apostolic See stemming from a lack of agreement among the electors. A renewed and complete regularization of ceremonial and Conclave organization can be found in Gregory XV's *Aeterni Patris* (November 15, 1621) and in the *Decet Romanum Pontificem* (March 12, 1622). With these documents the obligation was introduced that papal elections take place in the conclave and that voting for oneself was to be absolutely prohibited. The first original text composed of laws in this area is the Constitution *Vacante Sede Apostolica,* dated December 25, 1904. With this document, Pius X established the laws for the exercise and fulfillment of the College's greatest privilege — electing the Pope. It established the principle of the freedom of the Church from any type of interference from the secular world in choosing the Supreme Pontiff and contained innovative provisions relating to the secret balloting and a voting procedure involving a second poll.

John Paul II, referring to the ancient institution of the Conclave, states: "A careful historical examination confirms both the appropriateness of this institution, given the circumstances in which it originated and gradually took definitive shape, and its continued usefulness for the orderly, expeditious and proper functioning of the election itself, especially in times of tension and upheaval.

"Precisely for this reason, while recognizing that theologians and canonists of all times agree that this institution is not of its nature necessary for the valid election of the Roman Pontiff, I confirm by this Constitution that the Conclave is to continue in its essential structure; at the same time, I have made some modifications in order to adapt its procedures to present-day circumstances."

John Paul II established, for reasons relating to both comfort and functionality, that throughout the entire duration of the elections, voting cardinals have to reside at the *Domus Sanctae Marthae (House of St. Martha).* Build just to the southeast of St. Peter's Basilica, the building is inaccessible to non-Conclave members. John Paul II stressed the Conclave's nature of retreat and isolation, in light of the grave responsibility each of the members faces in selecting the supreme authority of the Catholic Church. Thus, even during the bus ride from the *Domus Sanctae Marthae* to the Vatican Apostolic Palace, the cardinals cannot be approached by anyone. In the introduction to the Constitution *Universi Dominici Gregis,* John Paul states: "I further confirm, by my apostolic authority, the duty of maintaining the strictest secrecy with regard to everything that directly or indirectly concerns the election process itself. Here too, however, I have wished to simplify the relative norms, reducing them to their essentials, in order to avoid confusion, doubts and even eventual problems of conscience on the part of those who have taken part in the election."

The total secrecy before, during and after the papal election is the responsibility of each of the participants and above all of the Chamberlain of the Sacred College. He is assisted from outside by the *"Sostituto"* (Deputy) of the Secretary of State, whose task it is to ensure that the Conclave is inaccessible to persons other than Conclave members and to make sure that no audiovisual equipment capable of recording or transmitting has been installed. The Commander of the Swiss Guards, the Prefect of the Pontifical Household and the Special Delegate of the Pontifical Commission for Vatican City have custody over the Conclave keys, and are responsible for the external locking of the Conclave.

Cardinals who are seriously ill can be accompanied by two Conclave secretaries (attendants, clerics or lay people) after swearing before the Cardinal Dean. From the moment voting begins, access to the Sistine Chapel is permitted only to the voters.

The site of the elections remains, as always, the Sistine Chapel in the Apostolic Palace, "where everything contributes to the increase of the awareness of the presence of God, to whom everyone will have to present himself one day to be judged."

The election begins with the celebration of the Mass *pro eligendo Papa* in the Basilica of St. Peter and with a procession from the Pauline Chapel to the Sistine Chapel of the Apostolic Palace. When the cardinal electors have arrived, the Cardinal Dean reads aloud the formula for the rite. Each cardinal swears to fully observe the provisions contained in the Apostolic Constitution *Universi Dominici Gregis* — to oppose any political pressure of whatever kind, to maintain the most rigorous silence on the electoral operations during and after the Conclave, and, if elected Pontiff, to defend the spiritual and temporal rights, as well as the freedom, of the Holy See. Immediately thereafter, the Master of Papal Liturgical Ceremonies signals the *extra omnes* (*"everyone outside"*) and the persons not taking part in the Conclave must leave the Sistine Chapel. After reciting the meditation on the difficult task at hand, the cleric chosen to deliver the meditation and the Master of the Papal Liturgical Ceremonies also leave.

John Paul II abolished the formality of elections *per acclamationem seu inspirationem* and *per compromissum*. In the case of the former, all cardinal electors, inspired by the Holy Spirit, would have had to proclaim unanimously and out loud the name of the future Pontiff. In the latter case, the College would have delegated the choice of the future Pontiff with a commitment to accept the decision to a group of cardinals composed of an odd number between nine and a maximum of 15. *Per acclamationem* was abolished because of the growth in numbers of electors, while *per compromissum* was done away with because of practical complications and problems of accountability. An election by secret ballot with a two-thirds majority has thus been, since 1996, "the only form in which voters can manifest their vote for the election of the Roman Pontiff." John Paul II holds: "Such a method, in fact, offers the greatest guarantees of clearness, linearity, simplicity, transparency and, above all, of effective and constructive participation of all the cardinals called to constitute the elective assembly for the Successor of Peter."

If a decision has not been reached after three days of voting, a 24-hour suspension period is called, during which time the electors can freely discuss with one another. After this, another seven votes are held, then a break, another seven votes, a break and then another seven votes. Following this, the College of Cardinals, upon the invitation of the Cardinal Chamberlain, can decide upon the means of proceeding, provided that the election result in at least a simple majority, including by voting only on the two names which in the ballot immediately preceding have received the greatest number of votes.

A positive outcome to the election interrupts the above-mentioned cycle. The ballots and any other writings must be burned before beginning a new phase.

The Cardinal Dean first asks for the consent of the elected and the name he has chosen. The Master of Papal Liturgical Ceremonies, in the presence of two ceremonial witnesses, then drafts the document of acceptance with the name of the pontiff and the Conclave ends.

Immediately (or, in the event the elected is not a bishop, after his episcopal ordination by the Cardinal Dean), the newly-elected becomes the Bishop of the Church of Rome and the Head of the Episcopal College. The chief of the Cardinal Deacons then announces the name of the newly-elected Pope to the faithful. The new Pope then immediately gives the *Urbi et Orbi* benediction from the Loggia of St. Peter's Basilica.

Karol Wojtyła, created a cardinal by Paul VI on June 27, 1967, was elected Pope on October 16, 1978, and took the name John Paul II. He was elected by 111 cardinals present in Conclave, in accordance with Paul VI's *Romano Pontifici eligendo* Constitution, written on October 1,1975.

A prayer — "Do not refuse!" — and a prediction — "You will lead the Church into the third millennium" — were the treasures Cardinal Stefan Wyszyński conferred on Karol Wojtyła just prior to the 1978 Conclave. The Polish primate Wyszyński, imprisoned by the Communist regime in 1953, was a mystic who performed healings through the intercession of Our Lady. His words endowed Wojtyla's pontificate with a special prophetic quality from the very outset.

This has indeed been an extraordinary pontificate. Signs of recognition come from all over the world acknowledging the marvelous deeds John Paul II has accomplished, and which we are sure he will continue to accomplish. He will never cease to surprise us, who admire him for his ability to communicate the true light, his capacity to support, encourage and comfort.

His example of courage, of love and of dedication to Christ and the Church is a profound inspiration for all mankind.

Cardinal František Tomašek, who was
persecuted under the communist
regime, and Czech president Vaclav
Havel greet the Pope upon his arrival
at Prague airport in 1990

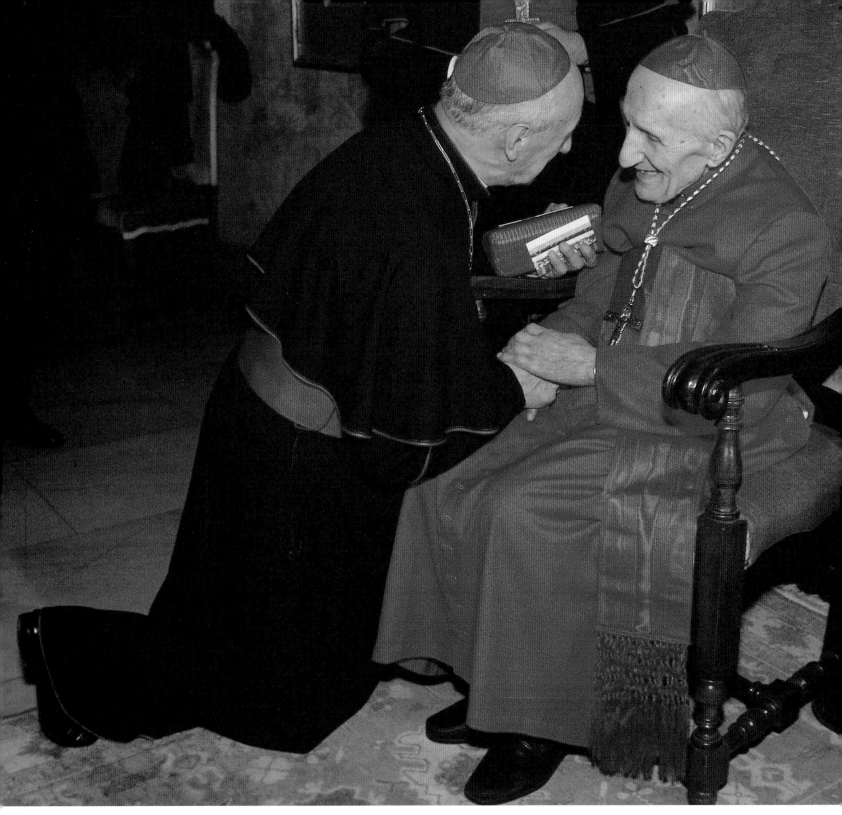

Cardinal Roger Etchegaray genuflects before
Cardinal Mikel Koliqi in a sign of profound
respect for the decades of imprisonment and
forced labor Koliqi endured under the Albanian
communist regime

Opposite page, top:
Cardinal Adam Kozłowiecki, S.J., who survived five
years in the concentration camps of Auschwitz and
Dachau, prays before the statue of St. Stanislao Kostka
in the church of Sant'Andrea al Quirinale

Bottom:
Cardinal Juan Jesus Ocampo Posadas. He was
shot to death at the airport of Guadalajara, Mexico, in
1993, after having publicly expressed his concern over
the spread of violence and crime in Mexico

A procession of cardinals in adoration of the Crucified One in St. Peter's Basilica during a Good Friday service

◀ The cardinals gathered for Mass in St. Peter's Basilica during the Extraordinary Consistory on April 7, 1991

A cardinal's coat-of-arms should include an image of a red hat with two side cords and 30 tassels of the same color, 15 on each side

Cardinals in the Synod Hall for the
Extraordinary Consistory of June 13, 1994

Above left: Euroclero tailor
Michele Ombroso shows the
cardinal's purple.
Left: new cardinals
Kazimierz Świątek and
Adolfo Antonio Suárez
Rivera, meet in the tailor's
shop several days before
the Consistory

Through photographs of several cardinals, we present the different phases in the preparation of the cardinal's clothing.

Cardinal Kazimierz Świątek tries on a garment in the tailor's shop

A tailor makes needed clothing adjustments for
Cardinal Zenon Grocholewski

Cardinal Juan Luis Cipriani Thorne puts on the red "*berretta*" and, in the photo below, he tries on the white damasque mitre

Cardinal Louis-Marie Billé

Cardinal Lehmann discusses his clothing while the Patriarch Stéphanos Ghattas II awaits his turn

The day before the Consistory, Cardinal Roberto Tucci receives his cardinal's clothing at his home

The day of the Consistory, February 21, 2001, Cardinal Giovanni Cheli reads his breviary as he awaits the beginning of the official ceremony

Cardinal Jorge María Mejía, one of the first to arrive, is helped in some final adjustments

On February 21, 2001, at 10.30 a.m., in St. Peter's Square, the Ordinary Public Consistory for the creation of 44 new cardinals begins with the celebration of the Liturgy of the Word

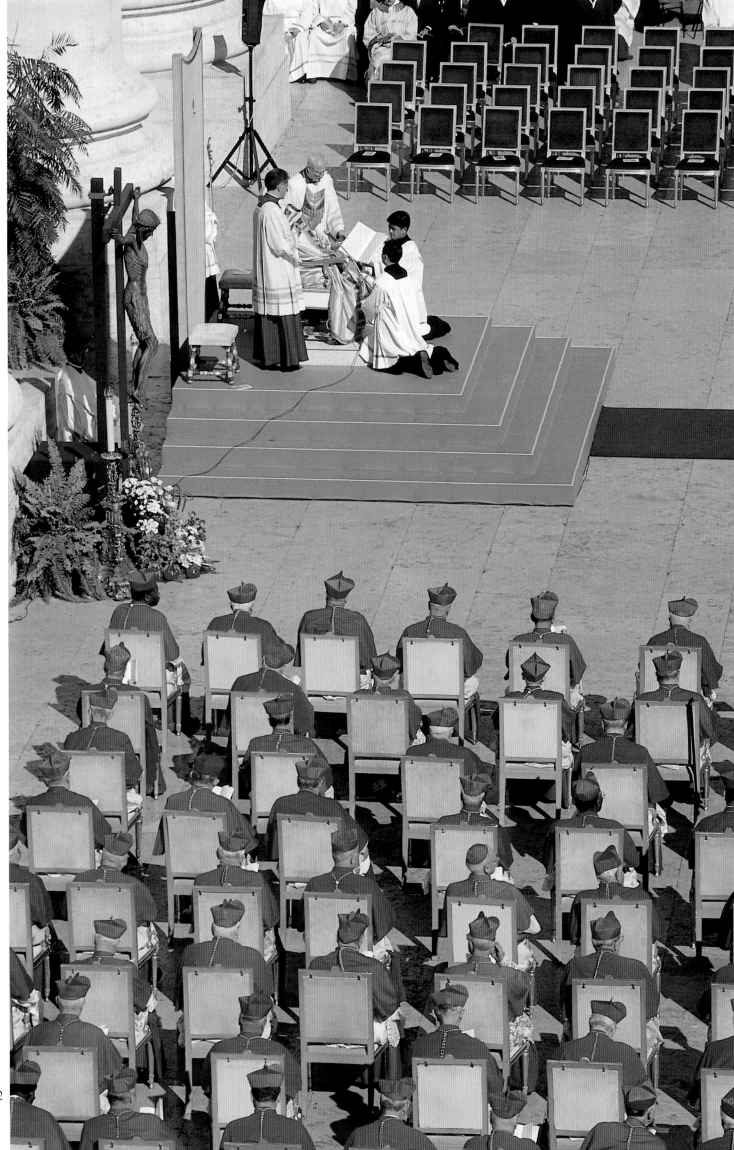

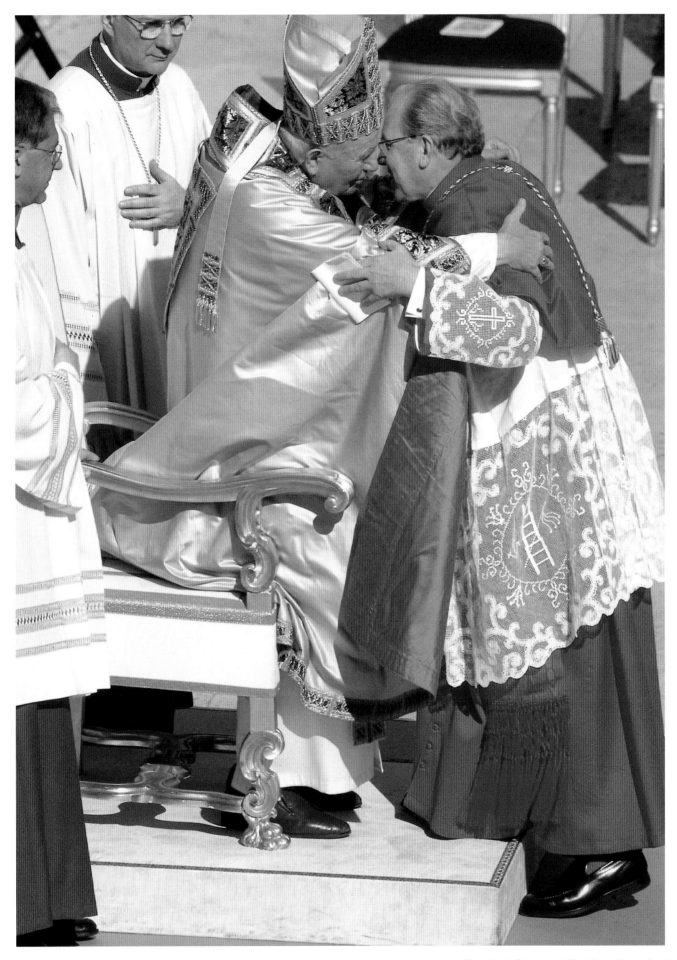

◀ In front of St. Peter's Basilica, Pope John Paul II, after the liturgical salutation, reads the formula of creation and solemnly announces the names of the new cardinals

Cardinal Giovanni Battista Re, after having thanked the Pope in the name of all the cardinals, embraces the pontiff

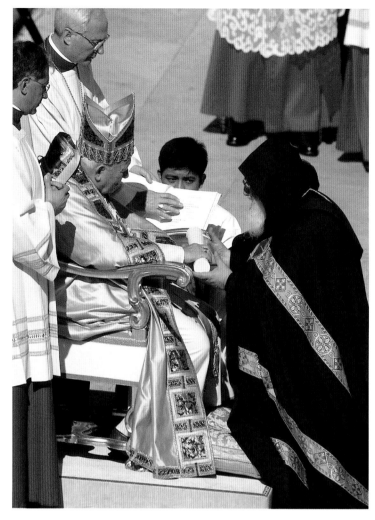
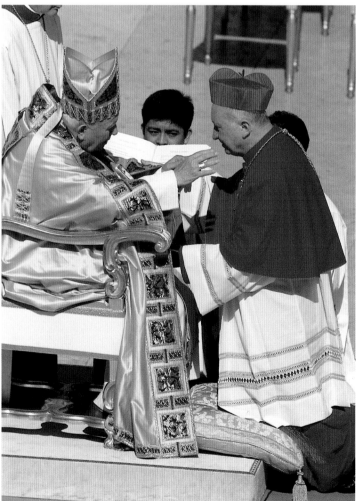

After the oath of loyalty and obedience to the Pope and his successors, Cardinal François Xavier Nguyên Van Thuân of Vietnam, like all of the new cardinals in the order of their creation, kneels before the Holy Father for the imposition of the cardinal's red hat

Cardinal Lubomyr Husar receives the bull announcing his creation as cardinal and his assignment to a Roman church, a sign of his participation in the Holy Father's pastoral solicitude for the city of Rome

John Paul II embraces Cardinal Marian Jaworski

Cardinal Francisco Álvares Martínez, after embracing the Pope, kisses the pontiff's hands in a gesture of gratitude

The Holy Father embraces the newly-created Cardinal Crescenzio Sepe

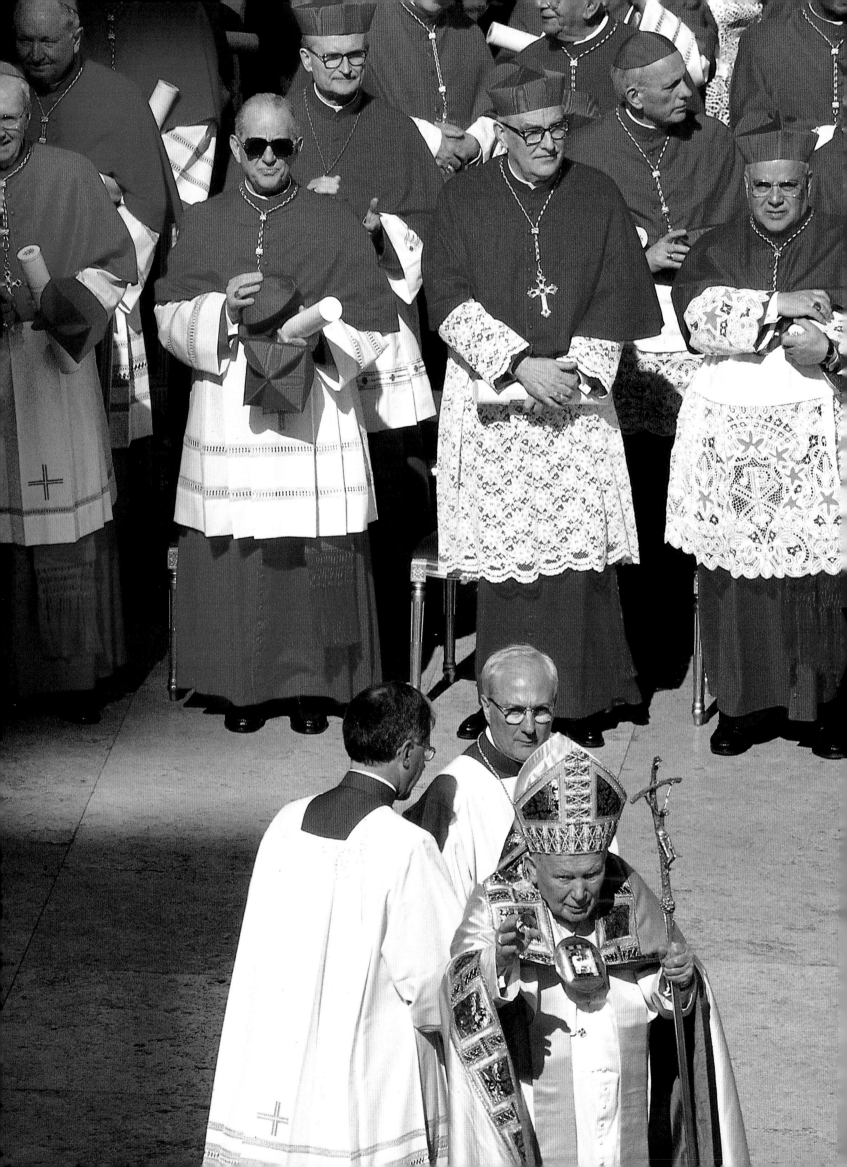

On the same day as the Consistory there are two hours of "courtesy visits" inside the Vatican, during which time the cardinals receive dozens of relatives, friends and well-wishers.
In the top photo, Cardinal Christoph Schönborn receives the family of Jean-Marie Guenois, a respected French journalist

Cardinal Juan Luis Cipriani Thorne receives Monsignor Javier Echeverria, Prelate of *Opus Dei*

Cardinal Angelo
Sodano and Cardinal
Severino Poletto take
advantage of a few
free moments to talk
things over

Cardinal Theodore
Edgar McCarrick, of
Washington, D.C.,
meets representatives
of the Jewish
community

Cardinal Roberto Tucci affectionately salutes some of those who have worked with him to prepare the Pope's trips over the years

Cardinals Desmond Connell, of Dublin, Ireland, and Avery Dulles, of the United States, greet cordially

During the ceremony of ▶ February 22, 2001, Cardinal Jãnis Pujats receives his ring, "sign of dignity, of pastoral solicitude and of still firmer communion with the See of Peter"

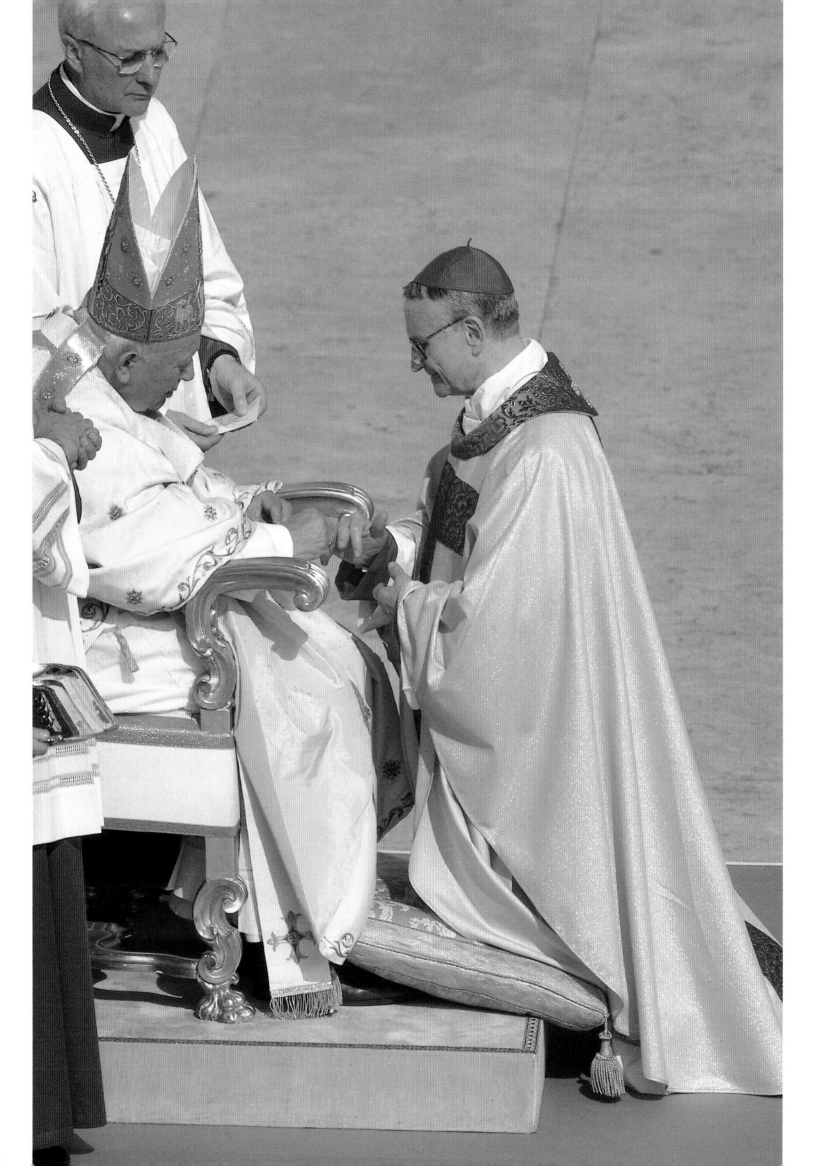

On February 22, 2001, John Paul II presides at the concelebration of the Eucharist with his new cardinals

The Pope's celebration of Mass with his new cardinals is made more solemn by the presence of the crucifix from the Sistine Chapel

In the following photographs, scenes of cardinals
"taking possession" of their titular churches in Rome

Cardinal Christoph Schönborn, of Vienna, Austria,
arrives at the church of Gesù Divin Lavoratore
("Jesus Divine Worker") and greets the children who
await him

Cardinal Pierre Eyt, from France, bends to kiss the crucifix in his titular church, SS. Trinità al Monte Pincio

Cardinal Adam Kozłowiecki imparts his blessing in his church, S. Andrea al Quirinale

Cardinal Jorge María Mejía prepares to
celebrate Mass in the church of
S. Girolamo della Carità

Cardinal Salvatore De Giorgi sitting in his titular church, S. Maria in Ara Coeli

Cardinal Carlo Furno signs the document receiving his titular church, the Diaconia del S. Cuore di Cristo Re

An aerial view of the *Domus Sanctae Marthae* as it is expanded and refurbished to serve as a residence for the college of cardinals

The *Domus Sanctae Marthae,* recently refurbished. It is generally used as a guest house for Vatican officials and visitors, but will also serve as the residence of all the cardinals during a Conclave

The *Domus Sanctae Marthae* is situated next to St. Peter's Basilica on the southeast side

Cardinal Juan Luis Cipriani Thorne in one of the ▶ rooms inside the *Domus Sanctae Marthae*

A view from the cupola of St. Peter's Basilica over the
Domus Sanctae Marthae and the Eternal City

An external view of the Sistine Chapel,
where papal elections are held

The famous *Last Judgment* of Michelangelo
on the wall of the Sistine Chapel

There are presently 183
Cardinals of whom 159 were
created by His Holiness John
Paul II.
In the pages which follow,
we present their photo
portraits and biographies
in the order of the
Consistories.

KÖNIG Franz
AUSTRIA

Born in Rabenstein, diocese of Sankt Pölten, on August 3, 1905; ordained October 29, 1933; named titular Bishop of Liviade July 3, 1952; consecrated August 31, 1952; promoted to Vienna May 10, 1956; created and proclaimed a cardinal by John XXIII in the Consistory of December 15, 1958; given the titular church of S. Eusebio; *President emeritus* of the Pontifical Council for Dialogue with Non-Believers; *Archbishop emeritus* of Vienna (retired September 16, 1985).

URSI Corrado

ITALY

Born in Andria July 26, 1908; ordained July 25, 1931; named Bishop of Nardò July 31, 1951; consecrated September 30, 1951; promoted to Acerenza November 30, 1961; transferred to Naples May 23, 1966; created and proclaimed a cardinal by Paul VI in the Consistory of June 26, 1967; given the titular church of S. Calisto; *Archbishop emeritus* of Naples (retired May 9, 1987).

BERTOLI Paolo

ITALY

Born in Poggio Garfagnana, archdiocese of Lucca, February 1, 1908; ordained August 15, 1930; named titular Bishop of Nicomedia March 24, 1952; consecrated May 11, 1952; created and proclaimed a cardinal by Paul VI in the Consistory of April 28, 1969; named Bishop of the title of suburbicarian see of Frascati, June 30, 1979; *Prefect emeritus* of the Congregation for the Causes of Saints; *Camerlengo* of the Holy Roman Church (retired March 25, 1985).

ODDI Silvio

ITALY

Born in Morfasso, diocese of Piacenza-Bobbio, November 14, 1910; ordained May 21, 1933; named titular Archbishop of Mesembria July 30, 1953; consecrated September 27, 1953; created and proclaimed a cardinal by Paul VI in the Consistory of April 28, 1969; given the titular church of S. Agata de' Goti; *Prefect emeritus of* the Congregation for the Clergy.

KIM SOU-HWAN Stephen

KOREA

Born in Taegu May 8, 1922; ordained September 15, 1951; named Bishop of Masan February 15, 1966; consecrated May 31, 1966; promoted to Seoul April 9, 1968; created and proclaimed a cardinal by Paul VI in the Consistory of April 28, 1969; given the titular church of San Felice da Cantalice a Centocelle; *Archbishop emeritus* of Seoul (retired April 3, 1998).

de ARAÚJO SALES Eugênio

BRAZIL

Born in Acari, diocese of Caicó, November 8, 1920; ordained November 21, 1943; named titular Bishop of Tibica June 1, 1954; consecrated August 15, 1954; promoted to São Salvador da Bahia October 29, 1968; created and proclaimed a cardinal by Paul VI in the Consistory of April 28, 1969; given the titular church of S. Gregorio VII, transferred to São Sebastião do Rio de Janeiro March 13, 1971; *Archbishop* of São Sebastião do Rio de Janeiro; *Ordinary* of Eastern-rite faithful in Brazil in absence of a local Ordinary.

WILLEBRANDS Johannes

THE NETHERLANDS

Born in Bovenkarspei, diocese of Haarlem, September 4, 1909; ordained May 26, 1934; named titular Bishop of Mauriana June 4, 1964; consecrated June 28, 1964; created and proclaimed a cardinal by Paul VI in the Consistory of April 28, 1969; given the titular church of S. Sebastiano alle Catacombe; nominated to Utrecht December 6, 1975 (retired December 3, 1983); *President emeritus* of the Pontifical Council for Christian Unity.

APONTE MARTÍNEZ Luis

PUERTO RICO

Born in Lajas, diocese of Mayagüez, August 4, 1922; ordained April 10, 1950; named titular Bishop of Lares July 23, 1960; consecrated October 12, 1960; succeeded to the see of Ponce November 18, 1963; promoted to San Juan de Puerto Rico November 4, 1964; created and proclaimed a cardinal by Paul VI in the Consistory of March 5, 1973; given the titular church of S. Maria Madre della Provvidenza a Monte Verde; *Archbishop emeritus* of San Juan de Puerto Rico (retired March 26, 1999).

PRIMATESTA Raúl Francisco

ARGENTINA

Born in Capilla del Señor, diocese of Zárate-Campana, April 14, 1919; ordained October 25, 1942; named titular Bishop of Tanais June 14, 1957; consecrated August 15, 1957; transferred to San Rafael June 12, 1961; promoted to Córdoba February 16, 1965; created and proclaimed a cardinal by Paul VI in the Consistory of March 5, 1973; given the titular church of S. Maria Vergine Addolorata in Piazza Buenos Aires; *Archbishop emeritus* of Córdoba (retired November 17, 1998).

PAPPALARDO Salvatore
ITALY

Born in Villafranca Sicula, diocese of Agrigento, September 23, 1918; ordained April 12, 1941; named titular Archbishop of Mileto December 7, 1965; consecrated January 16, 1966; transferred to Palermo October 17, 1970; created and proclaimed a cardinal by Paul VI in the Consistory of March 5, 1973; given the titular church of S. Maria Odigitria dei Siciliani; *Archbishop emeritus* of Palermo (retired April 4, 1996).

GONZÁLEZ MARTÍN Marcelo
SPAIN

Born in Villanubla, archdiocese of Valladolid, January 16, 1968; ordained June 29, 1941; named Bishop of Astorga December 31, 1960; consecrated March 5, 1961; promoted to titular Archbishop of Case Mediane February 21, 1966; succeeded to the see of Barcellona January 7, 1967; transferred to Toledo December 3, 1971; created and proclaimed cardinal by Paul VI in the Consistory of March 5, 1973; given the titular church of S. Agostino; *Archbishop emeritus* of Toledo (retired June 23, 1995).

OTUNGA Maurice Michael
KENYA

Born in Chebukwa, diocese of Kakamega, January 1923; ordained October 3, 1950; named titular Bishop of Tacape November 17, 1956; consecrated February 25, 1957; transferred to Kisii May 21, 1960; promoted titular Archbishop of Bomarzo November 15, 1969; succeeded to the see of Nairobi October 24, 1971; created and proclaimed a cardinal by Paul VI in the Consistory of March 5, 1973; given the titular church of S. Gregorio Barbarigo alle Tre Fontane; *Archbishop emeritus* of Nairobi (retired April 21, 1997*); Military Ordinary emeritus* of Kenya (retired August 29, 1997).

ARNS Paulo Evaristo, O.F.M.
BRAZIL

Born in Forquilhinha, diocese of Tubarão, September 14, 1921; ordained November 30, 1945; named titular Bishop of Respetta May 2, 1966; consecrated July 3, 1966; promoted to São Paulo October 22, 1970; created and proclaimed a cardinal by Paul VI in the Consistory of March 5, 1973; given the titular church of S. Antonio da Padova in Via Tuscolana; *Archbishop emeritus* of São Paulo (retired April 15, 1998).

TAOFINU'U Pio, S.M.
SAMOA

Born in Falealupo, archdiocese of Samoa-Apia, December 8, 1923; ordained December 8, 1954; named Bishop of Apia January 11, 1968; consecrated May 29, 1968; created and proclaimed a cardinal by Paul VI in the Consistory of March 5, 1973; given the titular church of S. Onofrio; promoted to Samoa-Apia and Tokelau September 10, 1982; *Archbishop* of Samoa-Apia.

ROSSI Opilio

ITALY

Born in New York March 14, 1910; ordained May 11, 1933; named titular Archbishop of Ancira November 21, 1953; consecrated December 27, 1953; created and proclaimed a cardinal by Paul VI in the Consistory of May 24, 1976; given the titular church of S. Lorenzo in Lucina; *President emeritus* of the Commission of Cardinals for the Pontifical Sanctuaries of Pompeii, Loreto and Bari.

SENSI Giuseppe Maria

ITALY

Born in Cosenza May 27, 1907; ordained December 21, 1929; elected titular Archbishop of Sardi May 21, 1955; consecrated July 24, 1955; created and proclaimed a cardinal by Paul VI in the Consistory of May 24, 1976; given the titular church of Regina Apostolorum.

ARAMBURU Juan Carlos

ARGENTINA

Born in Reducción, diocese of Villa de la Concepción del Río Cuarto, February 11, 1912; ordained October 28, 1934; named titular Bishop of Platea October 7, 1946; consecrated December 15, 1946; transferred to Tucumán August 28, 1953; promoted March 13, 1957; named titular Archbishop of Torri di Bizacena June 14, 1967; succeeded to the see of Buenos Aires April 22, 1975; created and proclaimed a cardinal by Paul VI in the Consistory of May 24, 1976; given the titular church of S. Giovanni Battista dei Fiorentini; *Archbishop emeritus* of Buenos Aires (retired July 10, 1990); *Ordinary* for the eastern rite faithful of Argentina in the absence of a local ordinary (retired November 20, 1990).

BAFILE Corrado
ITALY

Born in Aquila July 4, 1903; ordained April 11, 1936; named titular Archbishop of Antiochia di Pisidia February 13, 1960; consecrated March 19, 1960; created and proclaimed a cardinal by Paul VI in the Consistory of May 24, 1976; given the titular church of S. Maria in Portico; *Prefect emeritus* of the Congregation for the Causes of Saints.

THIANDOUM Hyacinthe
SENEGAL

Born in Poponguine, archdiocese of Dakar, February 2, 1921; ordained April 18, 1949; named Bishop of Dakar February 24, 1962; consecrated May 20, 1962; created and proclaimed a cardinal by Paul VI in the Consistory of May 24, 1976; given the titular church of S. Maria del Popolo; *Archbishop emeritus* of Dakar (resigned June 2, 2000).

SIN Jaime L.
PHILIPPINES

Born in New Washington, diocese of Kalibo, August 31, 1928; ordained April 3, 1954; named titular Bishop of Obba February 10, 1967; consecrated March 18, 1967; promoted Archbishop of Massa Lubrense January 15, 1972; succeeded to the see of Jaro October 8, 1972; transferred to Manila January 21, 1974; created and proclaimed a cardinal by Paul VI in the Consistory of May 24, 1976; given the titular church of S. Maria ai Monti; *Archbishop* of Manila.

BAUM William Wakefield
UNITED STATES

From the diocese of Kansas City-Saint Joseph; born in Dallas November 21, 1926; ordained May 12, 1951; named Bishop of Springfield-Cape Girardeau February 18, 1970; consecrated April 6, 1970; promoted to Washington March 5, 1973; created and proclaimed a cardinal by Paul VI in the Consistory of March 24, 1976; given the titular church of S. Croce in Via Flaminia; *Archbishop emeritus* of Washington (retired March 18, 1980); Major Penitentiary, April 6, 1990.

LORSCHEIDER Aloísio, O.F.M.
BRAZIL

Born in Estrela, archdiocese of Porto Alegre, October 8, 1924; ordained August 22, 1948; named Bishop of Santo Angelo February 3, 1962; consecrated May 20, 1962; promoted to Fortaleza March 26, 1973; created and proclaimed a cardinal by Paul VI in the Consistory of May 24, 1976; given the titular church of S. Pietro in Montorio; transferred to Aparecida July 12, 1995; *Archbishop* of Aparecida.

GANTIN Bernardin
BENIN

Born in Toffo, archdiocese of Cotonou, May 8, 1922; ordained January 14, 1951; named titular Bishop of Tipasa di Mauritania December 11, 1956; consecrated February 3, 1957; promoted to Cotonou January 5, 1960, created and proclaimed a cardinal by Paul VI in the Consistory of June 27, 1977; given the titular church of Sacro Cuore di Cristo Re; named Bishop of the suburbicarian see of Palestrina, September 29, 1986 and later of the suburbicarian see of Ostia, June 5 1993; *Prefect emeritus* of the Congregation for Bishops; *President emeritus* for the Pontifical Comission for Latin America; *Dean* of the College of Cardinals, June 5, 1993.

RATZINGER Joseph
GERMANY

Born in Marktl am Inn, diocese of Passau, April 16, 1927; ordained June 29, 1951; named Bishop of München und Freising March 24, 1977; consecrated May 28, 1977; created and proclaimed a cardinal by Paul VI in the Consistory of June 27, 1977; given the titular church of S. Maria Consolatrice al Tiburtino; named titular Bishop of the suburbicarian see of Velletri-Segni April 5, 1993; *Prefect* of the Congregation for the Doctrine of the Faith; *President* of the Pontifical Biblical Commission and the International Theological Commission, November 25, 1981; *Vice-Dean* of the College of Cardinals, November 6, 1998.

CAPRIO Giuseppe
ITALY

Born in Lapio, archdiocese of Benevento, November 15, 1914; ordained December 17, 1938; named titular Archbishop of Apollonia October 14, 1961; consecrated December 17, 1961; created and proclaimed a cardinal by John Paul II in the Consistory of June 30, 1979; given the titular church of S. Maria della Vittoria; *Grand Master* of the Equestrian Order of the Holy Sepulchre of Jerusalem (retired December, 1995); *President emeritus* of the Administration of the Patrimony of the Apostolic See.

CÉ Marco
ITALY

Born in Izano, diocese of Crema, July 8, 1925; ordained March 27, 1948; named titular Bishop of Vulturia April 22, 1970; consecrated May 17, 1970; promoted to patriarchal see of Venice December 7, 1978; created and proclaimed a cardinal by John Paul II in the Consistory of June 30, 1979; given the titular church of S. Marco; *Patriarch* of Venice.

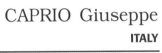

CORRIPIO AHUMADA Ernesto
MEXICO

Born in Tampico June 29, 1919; ordained October 25, 1942; named titular Bishop of Zapara December 27, 1952; consecrated March 19, 1953; transferred to Tampico February 25, 1956; promoted to Antequera July 25, 1967; transferred to Puebla de los Angeles March 8, 1976; transferred to Mexico July 19, 1977; created and proclaimed a cardinal by John Paul II in the Consistory of June 30, 1979; given the titular church of Immaculata al Tiburtino; *Archbishop emeritus* of Mexico (retired September 29, 1994).

ETCHEGARAY Roger
FRANCE

Born in Espelette, diocese of Bayonne, September 25, 1922; ordained July 13, 1947; named titular Bishop of Gemelle di Numidia March 29, 1969; consecrated May 27, 1969; promoted to Marsiglia December 22, 1970 (retired April 8, 1984); nominated Prelate of the "Mission de France" November 25, 1975 (retired April 23, 1982); created and proclaimed a cardinal by John Paul II in the Consistory of June 30, 1979; received the titular church of S. Leone I; named titular Bishop of the suburbicarian see of Porto-Santa Rufina, June 24, 1998; *President emeritus* of the Pontifical Council for Justice and Peace and of the Pontifical Council "Cor Unum."

95

CARTER Gerald Emmett
CANADA

Born in Montreal March 1, 1912; ordained May 22, 1937; named titular Bishop of Altiburo December 1, 1961; consecrated February 2, 1962; transferred to London February 17, 1964; promoted to Toronto April 27, 1978; created and proclaimed a cardinal by John Paul II in the Consistory of June 30, 1979; given the titular church of S. Maria in Traspontina; *Archbishop emeritus* of Toronto (retired March 17, 1990).

MACHARSKI Franciszek
POLAND

Born in Krakow May 20, 1927; ordained April 2, 1950; named Bishop of Krakow December 29, 1978; consecrated January 6, 1979; created and proclaimed a cardinal by John Paul II in the Consistory of June 30, 1979; given the titular church of S. Giovanni a Porta Latina; *Archbishop* of Krakow.

SABATTANI Aurelio
ITALY

Born in Casal Fiumanese, diocese of Imola, October 18, 1912; ordained July 26, 1935; named titular Archbishop of Giustiniana June 24, 1965; consecrated July 25, 1956; Prelate of Loreto (retired September 30, 1971); created and proclaimed a cardinal by John Paul II in the Consistory of February 2, 1983; given the titular church of S. Apolinare alle Terme Neroniane-Alessandrine; *Prefect emeritus* of the Supreme Tribunal for the Apostolic Signature; *Archpriest emeritus* of the Patriarchal Vatican Basilica; *Vicar General emeritus* of Vatican City State; *President emeritus* of the Reverend Fabric of St. Peter.

KUHARIĆ Franjo
CROATIA

Born in Pribiç, archdiocese of Zagreb, April 15, 1919; ordained July 15, 1945; named titular Bishop of Meta February 15, 1964; consecrated May 3, 1964; promoted to Zagreb June 16, 1970; created and proclaimed a cardinal by John Paul II in the Consistory of February 2, 1983; given the titular church of S. Girolamo dei Croati; *Archbishop emeritus* of Zagreb (retired July 5, 1997).

KITBUNCHU Michael Michai

THAILAND

Born in Samphran, archdiocese of Bangkok, January 25, 1929; ordained December 20, 1959; named Bishop of Bangkok December 18, 1972; consecrated June 3, 1973; created and proclaimed a cardinal by John Paul II in the Consistory of February 2, 1983; given the titular church of S. Lorenzo in Panisperna; *Archbishop* of Bangkok.

do NASCIMENTO Alexandre

ANGOLA

Born in Malanje March 1, 1925; ordained December 20, 1952; named Bishop of Malanje August 10, 1975; consecrated August 31, 1975; promoted to Lubango February 3, 1977; created and proclaimed a cardinal by John Paul II in the Consistory of February 2, 1983; given the titular church of S. Marco in Agro Laurentino; transferred to Luanda February 16, 1986; *Archbishop emeritus* of Luanda (retired January 23, 2001).

LÓPEZ TRUJILLO Alfonso

COLOMBIA

Born in Villahermosa, diocese of Líbano-Honda, November 8, 1935; ordained November 13, 1960; named titular Bishop of Boseta February 25, 1971; consecrated March 25, 1971; promoted Coadjuator of Medellín May 22, 1978; succeeded to the See of Medellín June 2, 1979; created and proclaimed a cardinal by John Paul II in the Consistory of February 2, 1983; given the titular church of S. Prisca; *Archbishop emeritus* of Medellín (retired January 9, 1991); *President* of the Pontifical Council for the Family, November 8, 1990.

DANNEELS Godfried

BELGIUM

Born in Kanegem, diocese of Brugges, June 4, 1933;
ordained August 17, 1957; named Bishop of Antwerp
November 4, 1977; consecrated December 18, 1977;
promoted to Mechelen-Brussels December 19, 1979;
created and proclaimed a cardinal by John Paul II in the
Consistory of February 2, 1982; given the titular church of
S. Anastasia; *Archbishop* of Mechelen-Brussels;
Military Ordinary for Belgium.

WILLIAMS Thomas Stafford

NEW ZEALAND

Born in Wellington March 20, 1930; ordained December 20,
1959; named Bishop of Wellington October 30, 1979;
consecrated December 20, 1979; created and proclaimed a
cardinal by John Paul II in the Consistory of February 2,
1983; given the titular church of Gesù Divin Maestro alla
Pineta Sacchetti; *Archbishop* of Wellington;
Military Ordinary for New Zealand.

MARTINI Carlo Maria, S.I.

ITALY

Born in Turin February 15, 1927; ordained July 13, 1952;
named Bishop of Milan December 29, 1979; consecrated
January 6, 1980; created and proclaimed a cardinal by John
Paul II in the Consistory of February 2, 1982; given the titular
church of S. Cecilia; *Archbishop* of Milan.

LUSTIGER Jean-Marie
FRANCE

Born in Paris September 17, 1926; ordained April 17, 1954; named Bishop of Orléans November 10, 1979; consecrated December 8, 1979; promoted to Paris January 31, 1981; created and proclaimed a cardinal by John Paul II in the Consistory of February 2, 1983; given the titular church of S. Luigi dei Francesi; *Archbishop* of Paris; *Ordinary* for the eastern rite faithful in France in absence of a local Ordinary.

GLEMP Józef
POLAND

Born in Inowroclaw, archdiocese of Gniezno, December 18, 1929; ordained May 25, 1956; named Bishop of Warmia March 4, 1979; consecrated April 21, 1979; promoted to Gniezno July 7, 1981; named Archbishop of Warsaw March 25, 1992; created and proclaimed a cardinal by John Paul II in the Consistory of February 2, 1983; given the titular church of S. Maria in Trastevere; *Archbishop* of Warsaw; *Ordinary* for the eastern rite faithful in Poland in absence of a local Ordinary.

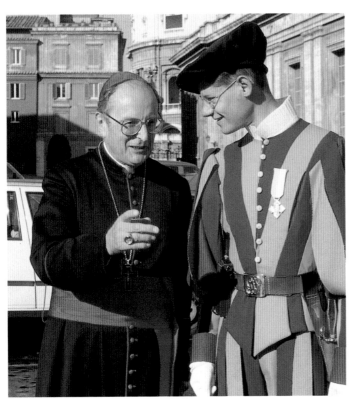

MEISNER Joachim
GERMANY

Born in Breslau December 25, 1933; ordained December 22, 1962; named titular Bishop of Vina March 17, 1975; consecrated May 17, 1975; transferred to Berlin April 22, 1980; created and proclaimed a cardinal by John Paul II in the Consistory of February 2, 1983; given the titular church of S. Pudenziana; promoted to Köln (Cologne) December 20, 1988; *Archbishop* of Köln (Cologne) .

LOURDUSAMY D. Simon

INDIA

Born in Kalleri, archdiocese of Pondicherry and Cuddalore, February 5, 1924; ordained December 21, 1951; named titular Bishop of Sozusa of Libya July 2, 1962; consecrated August 22, 1962; promoted to titular Archbishop of Filippi November 9, 1964; succeeded to the see of Bangalore January 11, 1968; created and proclaimed a cardinal by John Paul II in the Consistory of May 25, 1985; given the titular church of S. Maria delle Grazie alle Fornaci fuori Porta; *Prefect emeritus* of the Congregation for Eastern Churches.

ARINZE Francis

NIGERIA

Born in Eziowelle, archdiocese of Onitsha, November 1, 1932; ordained November 23, 1958; named titular Bishop of Fissiana July 6, 1965; consecrated August 29, 1965; promoted to Onitsha June 26, 1967; created and proclaimed a cardinal by John Paul II in the Consistory of May 25, 1985; given the titular church of S. Giovanni della Pigna; *President* of the Pontifical Council for Interreligious Dialogue, May 27, 1985.

FRESNO LARRAÍN Juan Francisco
CHILE

Born in Santiago del Chile July 26, 1914; ordained December 18, 1937; named Bishop of Copiapó June 15, 1958; consecrated August 15, 1958; promoted to La Serena July 28, 1967; transferred to Santiago del Cile May 3, 1983; created and proclaimed a cardinal by John Paul II in the Consistory of May 25, 1985; given the titular church of S. Maria Immaculata di Lourdes a Boccea; *Archbishop emeritus* of Santiago del Cile (retired March 30, 1990).

INNOCENTI Antonio
ITALY

Born in Poppi, diocese of Fiesole, August 23, 1915; ordained July 17, 1938; named titular Archbishop of Eclano December 15, 1967; consecrated February 18, 1968; created and proclaimed a cardinal by John Paul II in the Consistory of May 25, 1985; given the titular church of S. Maria in Aquiro; *Prefect emeritus* of the Congregation for Clergy; *President emeritus* of the Pontifical Commission for Conservation of the Artistic and Historical Patrimony of the Church; *President emeritus* of the Pontifical Commission "Ecclesia Dei".

OBANDO BRAVO Miguel, S.D.B
NICARAGUA

Born in La Libertad (Chontales), diocese of Juigalpa, February 2, 1926; ordained August 10, 1958; named titular Bishop of Puzia di Bizacena January 18, 1968; consecrated March 31, 1968; promoted to Managua February 16, 1970; created and proclaimed a cardinal by John Paul II in the Consistory of May 25, 1985; given the titular church of S. Giovanni Evangelista a Spinaceto; *Archbishop* of Managua.

MAYER Paul Augustin, O.S.B.
GERMANY

Born in Altötting, diocese of Passau, May 23, 1911; ordained August 25, 1935; named titular Archbishop of Satriano January 6, 1972; consecrated February 13, 1972; created and proclaimed a cardinal by John Paul II in the Consistory of May 25, 1985; given the titular church of S. Anselmo all'Aventino; *Prefect emeritus* of the Congregation for Divine Worship and Discipline of the Sacraments; *President emeritus* of the Pontifical Commision "Ecclesia Dei."

SUQUÍA GOICOECHEA Angel
SPAIN

Born in Zaldivia, diocese of San Sebastián, October 2, 1916; ordained July 7, 1940; named titular Bishop of Almería May 17, 1966; consecrated July 16, 1966; transferred to Málaga November 28, 1969; promoted to Santiago de Compostela April 13, 1973; transferred to Madrid April 12, 1983; created and proclaimed a cardinal by John Paul II in the Consistory of May 25, 1985; given the titular church of Gran Madre di Dio; *Archbishop emeritus* of Madrid (retired July 28, 1994).

VIDAL Ricardo J.
PHILIPPINES

Born in Mogpog, diocese of Boac, February 6, 1931; ordained March 17, 1956; named titular Bishop of Claterna September 10, 1971; consecrated November 30, 1971; promoted to Lipa August 22, 1973; nominated Coadjutor of Cebu April 13, 1981; succeeded to the see of Cebu August 24, 1982; created and proclaimed a cardinal by John Paul II in the Consistory of May 25, 1985; given the titular church of Ss. Pietro and Paolo in Via Ostiense; *Archbishop* of Cebu.

GULBINOWICZ Henryk Roman
POLAND

Born in Sukiškès, Archdiocese of Vilnius, October 17, 1928; ordained June 18, 1950; named titular Bishop of Acci January 12, 1970; consecrated February 8, 1970; promoted to Wrocław January 3, 1968; created and proclaimed a cardinal by John Paul II in the Consistory of May 25, 1985; given the titular church of Immacolata Concezione di Maria a Grottarossa; *Archbishop* of Wrocław.

TZADUA Paulos
ETHIOPIA

Born in Addifini, eparchy of Asmara, August 25, 1921; ordained March 12, 1944; named titular Bishop of Abila of Palestina March 1, 1973; consecrated May 20, 1973; promoted to Addis Abeba February 24, 1977; created and proclaimed a cardinal by John Paul II in the Consistory of May 25, 1985; given the titular church of Ss. Nome di Maria in Via Latina; *Archbishop emeritus* of Addis Abeba (retired September 11, 1998).

TOMKO Jozef
SLOVAKIA

Born in Udavské, archdiocese of Košice, March 11, 1924; ordained March 12, 1949; named titular Archbishop of Doclea February 12, 1979; consecrated September 15, 1979; created and proclaimed a cardinal by John Paul II in the Consistory of May 25, 1985; given the titular church of S. Sabina; *Prefect emeritus* of the Congregation for the Evangelization of Peoples; *Grand Chancellor* of the Pontifical Urbaniana University.

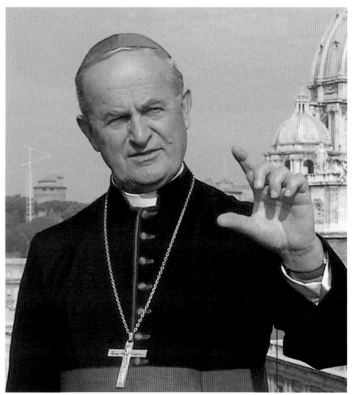

DESKUR Andrzej Maria
POLAND

Born in Sancygniów, diocese of Kielce, February 29, 1924; ordained August 20, 1950; named titular Bishop of Tene June 17, 1974; consecrated June 30, 1974; promoted to Archbishop February 15, 1980; created and proclaimed a cardinal by John Paul II in the Consistory of May 25, 1985; given the titular church of S. Cesareo in Palatio; *President emeritus* of the Pontifical Council for Social Communications.

POUPARD Paul
FRANCE

Born in Bouzillé, diocese of Angers, August 30, 1930; ordained December 18, 1954; named titular Bishop of Usula February 2, 1979; consecrated April 6, 1979; promoted Archbishop June 27, 1980; created and proclaimed a cardinal by John Paul II in the Consistory of May 25, 1985; given the titular church of S. Prassede; *President* of the Pontifical Council for Culture, April 19, 1988.

VACHON Louis-Albert
CANADA

Born in Saint-Frédéric-de-Beauce, archdiocese of Québec, February 4, 1912; ordained June 11, 1938; named titular Bishop of Mesarfelta April 4, 1977; consecrated May 14, 1977; promoted to Québec March 20, 1981; created and proclaimed a cardinal by John Paul II in the Consistory of May 25, 1985; given the titular church of S. Paolo della Croce a "Corviale"; *Archbishop emeritus* of Québec (retired March 17, 1990).

CASTILLO LARA Rosalio José, S.D.B.
VENEZUELA

Born in San Casimiro, diocese of Maracay, September 4, 1922; ordained September 4, 1949; named titular Bishop of Precausa March 26, 1973; consecrated May 24, 1973; promoted to Archbishop May 26, 1982; created and proclaimed a cardinal by John Paul II in the Consistory of May 25, 1985; given the titular church of Nostra Signora di Coromoto in S. Giovanni di Dio; *President emeritus* of the Administration of the Patrimony of the Holy See; *President emeritus* of the Pontifical Commision for the Vatican City State.

WETTER Friedrich
GERMANY

Born in Landau, diocese of Speyer, February 20, 1928; ordained October 10, 1953; named Bishop of Speyer May 28, 1968; consecrated June 29, 1968; promoted to München und Freising October 28, 1982; created and proclaimed a cardinal by John Paul II in the Consistory of May 25, 1985; given the titular church of S. Stefano al Monte Celio; *Archbishop* of München und Freising (Munich and Freising).

PIOVANELLI Silvano
ITALY

Born in Ronta di Mugello, archdiocese of Florence, February 21, 1924; ordained July 13, 1947; named titular Bishop of Tubune di Mauritania May 28, 1982; consecrated June 24, 1982; promoted to Florence March 18, 1983; created and proclaimed a cardinal by John Paul II in the Consistory of May 25, 1985; given the titular church of S. Maria delle Grazie in Via Trionfale; *Archbishop emeritus* of Florence.

SIMONIS Adrianus Johannes
THE NETHERLANDS

Born in Lisse, diocese of Rotterdam, November 26, 1931; ordained June 15, 1957; named Bishop of Rotterdam December 29, 1970; consecrated March 20, 1971; promoted Coadjutor of Utrecht June 27, 1983; succeeded to the see of Utrecht December 3, 1983; created and proclaimed a cardinal by John Paul II in the Consistory of May 25, 1985; given the titular church of San Clemente; *Archbishop* of Utrecht.

GAGNON Edouard, P.S.S.
CANADA

Born in Port-Daniel, diocese of Gaspé, January 15, 1918; ordained August 15, 1940; named Bishop of Saint Paul in Alberta February 19, 1969; consecrated March 25, 1969; promoted titular archbishop of Giustiniana July 7, 1983; created and proclaimed a cardinal by John Paul II in the Consistory of May 25, 1985; given the titular church of S. Marcello; *President emeritus* of the Pontifical Council for the Family; *President emeritus* of the Pontifical Commission for the International Eucharistic Conference.

STICKLER Alfons Maria, S.D.B.
AUSTRIA

Born in Neunkirchen, archdiocese of Vienna, August 23, 1910; ordained March 27, 1937; named titular Archbishop of Bolsena September 8, 1983; consecrated November 1, 1983; created and proclaimed a cardinal by John Paul II in the Consistory of May 25, 1985; given the titular church of S. Giorgio in Velabro; *Archivist* and *Librarian emeritus* of the Holy Roman Church.

LAW Bernard Francis
UNITED STATES

Born in Torreón, Mexico November 4, 1931; ordained May 21, 1961; named Bishop of Springfield-Cape Girardeau October 22, 1973; consecrated December 5, 1973; promoted to Boston January 11, 1984; created and proclaimed a cardinal by John Paul II in the Consistory of May 25, 1985; given the titular church of S. Susanna; *Archbishop* of Boston.

BIFFI Giacomo
ITALY

Born in Milan June 13, 1928; ordained December 23, 1950; named titular Bishop of Fidene December 7, 1975; consecrated January 11, 1976; promoted to Bologna April 19, 1984; created and proclaimed a cardinal by John Paul II in the Consistory of May 25, 1985; given the titular church of Ss. Giovanni Evangelista e Petronio; *Archbishop* of Bologna.

MARTÍNEZ SOMALO Eduardo

SPAIN

Born in Baños de Río Tobía, diocese of Calahorra y La Calzada-Logroño, March 31, 1927; ordained March 19, 1960; named titular Archbishop of Tagora November 12, 1975; consecrated December 13, 1975; created and proclaimed a cardinal by John Paul II in the Consistory of June 28, 1988; given the titular church of Ss. Nome di Gesù; *Prefect* of the Congregation for the Institutes of Consecrated Life and the Societies of Apostolic Life, January 21, 1992; *Camerlengo* of the Holy Roman Church, April 5, 1993.

SILVESTRINI Achille

ITALY

Born in Brisighella, diocese of Faenza-Modigliana, October 25, 1923; ordained July 13, 1946; named titular Archbishop of Novaliciana May 4, 1979; consecrated May 27, 1979; created and proclaimed a cardinal by John Paul II in the Consistory of June 28, 1988; given the titular church of S. Benedetto fuori Porta S. Paolo; *Prefect emeritus* of the Congregation for Oriental Churches.

FELICI Angelo
ITALY

Born in Segni July 26, 1919; ordained April 4, 1942; named titular Archbishop of Cesariana July 22, 1967; consecrated September 24, 1967; created and proclaimed a cardinal by John Paul II in the Consistory of June 28, 1988; given the titular church of Ss. Biagio e Carlo ai Catinari; *Prefect emeritus* of the Congregation for the Causes of Saints; *President emeritus* of the Pontifical Commission "Ecclesia Dei."

FALCÃO FREIRE José
BRAZIL

Born in Ererê, diocese of Limoeirio do Norte, October 23, 1925; ordained June 19, 1949; named titular Bishop of Vardimissa April 24, 1967; consecrated June 17, 1967; succeeded to the see of Limoeiro do Norte August 19, 1967; promoted to Teresina November 25, 1971; transferred to Brasília February 15, 1984; created and proclaimed a cardinal by John Paul II in the Consistory of June 28, 1988; given the titular church of S. Luca in Via Prenestina; *Archbishop* of Brasília.

GIORDANO Michele
ITALY

Born in S. Arcangelo, diocese of Tursi-Lagonegro, September 26, 1930; ordained July 5, 1953; named titular Bishop of Lari Castello December 23, 1971; consecrated February 5, 1972; promoted to Matera e Irsina June 12, 1974; transferred to Naples May 9, 1987; created and proclaimed a cardinal by John Paul II in the Consistory of June 28, 1988; given the titular church of S. Gioacchino ai Prati di Castello; *Archbishop* of Naples.

SANTOS Alexandre José Maria dos, O.F.M.
MOZAMBIQUE

Born in Zavala, diocese of Inhambane, March 18, 1924; ordained June 25, 1953; named Bishop of Maputo December 23, 1974; consecrated March 9, 1975; created and proclaimed a cardinal by John Paul II in the Consistory of June 28, 1988; given the titular church of S. Frumenzio ai Prati Fiscali; *Archbishop* of Maputo.

CANESTRI Giovanni
ITALY

Born in Castelspina, diocese of Alessandria, September 30, 1918; ordained April 12, 1941; named titular Bishop of Tenedo July 8, 1961; conescrated July 30, 1961; transferred to Tortona January 7, 1971; named titular Archbishop of Monterano February 8, 1975; transferred to Cagliari March 22, 1984; transferred to Genova July 6, 1987; created and proclaimed a cardinal by John Paul II in the Consistory of June 28, 1988; given the titular church of S. Andrea della Valle; *Archbishop emeritus* of Genova (retired April 20, 1995).

JAVIERRE ORTAS Antonio María, S.D.B.
SPAIN

Born in Siétamo, diocese of Huesca, February 21, 1921; ordained April 24, 1949; named titular Archbishop of Meta May 20, 1976; consecrated June 29, 1976; created and proclaimed a cardinal by John Paul II in the Consistory of June 28, 1988; given the titular church of S. Maria Liberatrice a Monte Testaccio; *Prefect emeritus* of the Congregation for Divine Worship and the Discipline of the Sacraments.

PIMENTA Simon Ignatius
INDIA

Born in Marol, archdiocese of Bombay, March 1, 1920; ordained December 21, 1949; named titular Bishop of Bocconia June 5, 1971; consecrated June 29, 1971; promoted Coadjutor of Bombay February 26, 1977; succeeded to the see of Bombay September 11, 1978; created and proclaimed a cardinal by John Paul II in the Consistory of June 28, 1988; given the titular church of S. Maria "Regina Mundi" a Torre Spaccata; *Archbishop emeritus* of Bombay (retired November 8, 1996).

NEVES MOREIRA Lucas O.P.
BRAZIL

Born in São João del Rei September 16, 1925; ordained July 9, 1950; named titular Bishop of Feradi maggiore June 9, 1967; consecrated August 26, 1976; promoted to Archbishop October 15, 1979; transferred to Vescovio January 3, 1987; transferred to São Salvador da Bahia July 9, 1987; created and proclaimed a cardinal by John Paul II in the Consistory of June 28, 1988; named titular Bishop of the suburbicarian see of Sabina-Poggio Mirteto, retaining *in commendam* the title of Ss. Bonifacio e Alessio, June 25, 1998; *Archbishop emeritus* of São Salvador da Bahia (retired June 25, 1998); *Prefect emeritus* of the Congregation for Bishops; *President emeritus* for the Pontifical Commission for Latin America.

CLANCY Edward Bede
AUSTRALIA

Born in Lithgow, diocese of Bathurst, December 13, 1923; ordained July 23, 1949; named titular Bishop of Árd Carna October 25, 1973; consecrated January 19, 1974; promoted to Canberra November 24, 1978; transferred to Sydney February 12, 1983; created and proclaimed a cardinal by John Paul II in the Consistory of June 28, 1988; given the titular church of S. Maria in Vallicella; *Archbishop* of Sydney (retired March 26, 2001).

HICKEY James Aloysius
UNITED STATES

Born in Midland, diocese of Saginaw, October 11, 1920; ordained June 15, 1946; named titular Bishop of Taraqua February 18, 1967; consecrated April 14, 1967; transferred to Cleveland May 31, 1974; promoted to Washington June 17, 1980; created and proclaimed a cardinal by John Paul II in the Consistory of June 28, 1988; given the titular church of S. Maria Madre del Redentore a Tor Bella Monaca; *Archbishop emeritus* of Washington (retired November 21, 2000).

SZOKA Edmund Casimir
UNITED STATES

Born in Grand Rapids September 14, 1927; ordained June 5, 1954; named Bishop of Gaylord June 11, 1971; consecrated July 20, 1971; promoted to Detroit March 21, 1981; created and proclaimed a cardinal by John Paul II in the Consistory of June 28, 1988; given the titular church of Ss. Andrea e Gregorio al Monte Celio; *Archbishop emeritus* of Detroit (retired April 28, 1990); *President* of the Pontifical Commission for Vatican City State, October 14, 1997; *President* of the Governature of Vatican City State, February 22, 2001.

PASKAI László, O.F.M.

HUNGARY

Born in Szeged May 8, 1927; ordained March 3, 1951; named titular Bishop of Bavagaliana March 2, 1978; consecrated April 5, 1978; transferred to Veszprém March 31, 1979; promoted Coadjutor of Kalocsa April 5, 1982; transferred to Esztergom March 3, 1987; created and proclaimed a cardinal by John Paul II in the Consistory of June 28, 1988; given the titular church of S. Teresa al Corso d'Italia; *Archbishop* of Esztergom-Budapest.

TUMI Christian Wiyghan

CAMEROON

Born in Kikaikelaki, diocese of Kumbo, October 15, 1930; ordained April 17, 1966; named Bishop of Yagoua December 6, 1979; consecrated January 6, 1980; promoted Coadjutor of Garoua November 19, 1982; succeeded to the see of Garoua March 17, 1984; created and proclaimed a cardinal by John Paul II in the Consistory of June 28, 1988; given the titular church of Ss. Martiri dell'Uganda a Poggio Ameno; transferred to Douala August 31, 1991; *Archbishop* of Douala.

GROËR Hans Hermann, O.S.B.
AUSTRIA

Born in Vienna October 13, 1919; ordained April 12, 1942; named Bishop of Vienna July 15, 1986; consecrated September 14, 1986; created and proclaimed a cardinal by John Paul II in the Consistory of June 28, 1988; given the titular church of Ss. Gioacchino ed Anna al Tuscolano; *Archbishop emeritus* of Vienna (retired September 14, 1995).

MARGÉOT Jean
MAURITIUS

Born in Quatre-Bornes, diocese of Port-Louis, February 3, 1916; ordained December 17, 1938; named Bishop of Port-Louis February 6, 1969; consecrated May 4, 1969; created and proclaimed a cardinal by John Paul II in the Consistory of June 28, 1988; given the titular church of S. Gabriele Arcangelo all'Acqua Traversa; *Bishop emeritus* of Port-Louis (retired February 15, 1993).

WU CHENG-CHUNG John Baptist
CHINA

Born in Shui-tsai, diocese of Kaying, March 26, 1927; ordained July 6, 1952; named Bishop of Hong Kong April 5, 1975; consecrated July 25, 1975; created and proclaimed a cardinal by John Paul II in the Consistory of June 28, 1988; given the titular church of Beata Vergine Maria del Monte Carmelo a Mostacciano; *Bishop* of Hong Kong.

SODANO Angelo
ITALY

Born in Isola d'Asti, diocese of Asti, November 23, 1927; ordained September 23, 1950; named titular Archbishop of Nova di Cesare November 30, 1977; consecrated January 15, 1978; Pro-Secretary of State, December 1, 1990; created and proclaimed a cardinal by John Paul II in the Consistory of June 28, 1991; named titular Bishop of the suburbicarian see of Albano, January 10, 1994; *Secretary of State*, June 29, 1991.

TODEA Alexandru
ROMANIA

Born in Teleac, archparish of Făgăraş şi Alba Iulia, June 5, 1912; ordained March 25, 1939; named titular Bishop of Cesaropoli July 4, 1950; consecrated November 19, 1950; promoted to Făgăraş şi Alba Iulia March 14, 1990; created and proclaimed a cardinal by John Paul II in the Consistory of June 28, 1991; given the titular church of S. Atanasio in Via Tiburtina; *Archbishop emeritus* of Făgăraş şi Alba Iulia (retired July 20, 1994).

ETSOU-NZABI-BAMUNGWABI
Frédéric, C.I.C.M.
CONGO

Born in Mazalonga, diocese of Lisala, December 3, 1930; ordained July 13, 1958; named titular Archbishop of Menefessi July 8, 1976; consecrated November 7, 1976; succeeded to the see of Mbandaka-Bikoro November 1977; transferred to Kinshasa July 7, 1990; created and proclaimed a cardinal by John Paul II in the Consistory of June 28, 1991; given the titular church of S. Lucia in Piazza d'Armi; *Archbishop* of Kinshasa.

LÓPEZ RODRÍGUEZ Nicolás de Jesús
DOMINICAN REPUBLIC

Born in Barranca, diocese of Las Vegas, October 31, 1936; ordained March 18, 1961; named Bishop of San Francisco de Macorís January 16, 1978; consecrated February 25, 1978; promoted to Santo Domingo November 15, 1981; created and proclaimed a cardinal by John Paul II in the Consistory of June 28, 1991; given the titular church of S. Pio X alla Balduina; *Archbishop* of Santo Domingo; *Military Ordinary* for the Dominican Republic.

MAHONY Roger Michael
UNITED STATES

Born in Hollywood, archdiocese of Los Angeles, February 27, 1936; ordained May 1, 1962; named titular Bishop of Tamascani January 7, 1975; consecrated March 19, 1975; transferred to Stockton February 15, 1980; promoted to Los Angeles July 16, 1985; created and proclaimed a cardinal by John Paul II in the Consistory of June 28, 1991; given the titular church of Ss. Quattro Coronati; *Archbishop* of Los Angeles.

BEVILACQUA Anthony Joseph
UNITED STATES

Born in Brooklyn June 17, 1923; ordained June 11, 1949; named titular Bishop of Acque Albe di Bizacena October 4, 1980; consecrated November 24, 1980; transferred to Pittsburgh October 10, 1983; promoted to Philadelphia February 11, 1988; created and proclaimed a cardinal by John Paul II in the Consistory of June 28, 1991; given the titular church of Ss. Redentore e S. Alfonso in Via Merulana; *Archbishop* of Philadelphia.

SALDARINI Giovanni
ITALY

Born in Cantù, archdiocese of Milan, December 11, 1924; ordained May 31, 1947; named titular Bishop of Gaudiaba November 10, 1984; consecrated December 7, 1984; promoted to Turin January 31, 1989; created and proclaimed a cardinal by John Paul II in the Consistory of June 28, 1991; given the titular church of S. Cuore di Gesù a Castro Pretorio; *Archbishop emeritus* of Turin (retired June 19, 1999).

DALY Cahal Brendan
IRELAND

Born in Loughguile, diocese of Down and Connor, October 1, 1917; ordained June 22, 1941; named Bishop of Ardagh May 26, 1967; consecrated July 16, 1976; transferred to Down and Connor August 24, 1982; promoted to Armagh November 6, 1990; created and proclaimed a cardinal by John Paul II in the Consistory of June 28, 1991; given the titular church of S. Patrizio; *Archbishop emeritus* of Armagh (retired October 1, 1996).

RUINI Camillo

ITALY

Born in Sassuolo, diocese of Reggio Emilia-Guastalla, February 19, 1931; ordained December 8, 1954; named titular Bishop of Nepte May 16, 1983; consecrated June 29, 1983; promoted Archbishop January 17, 1991; *Pro-Vicar General* of His Holiness for the Diocese of Rome and *Archpriest* of the Patriarchal Lateran Basilica, January 17, 1991; created and proclaimed a cardinal by John Paul II in the Consistory of June 28, 1991; given the titular church of S. Agnese fuori le mura; *Vicar General* of His Holiness for the diocese of Rome and *Archpriest* of the Patriarchal Lateran Basilica; *Grand Chancellor* of the Pontifical Lateran University; *President emeritus* of the "Peregrinatio ad Petri Sedem".

KOREC Ján Chryzostom, S.I.

SLOVAKIA

Born in Bošany, Diocese of Nitra, January 22, 1924; ordained October 1, 1950; consecrated August 24, 1951; nominated to Nitra February 6, 1990; created and proclaimed a cardinal by John Paul II in the Consistory of June 28, 1991; given the titular church of Ss. Fabiano e Venanzio a Villa Fiorelli; *Bishop* of Nitra.

SCHWERY Henri

SWITZERLAND

Born in Saint-Léonard, diocese of Sion, June 14, 1932; ordained July 7, 1975; named Bishop of Sion July 22, 1977; consecrated September 17,1977; created and proclaimed a cardinal by John Paul II in the Consistory of June 28, 1991; given the titular church of Ss. Protomartiri in Via Aurelia Antica; *Bishop emeritus* of Sion (retired April 1, 1995).

STERZINSKY Georg Maximilian

GERMANY

Born in Warlack, archdiocese of Warmia, February 9, 1936; ordained June 29, 1960; named Bishop of Berlin May 28, 1989; consecrated September 9, 1989; promoted June 27, 1994; created and proclaimed a cardinal by John Paul II in the Consistory of June 28, 1991; given the titular church of S. Giuseppe all'Aurelio; *Archbishop* of Berlin.

LAGHI Pio

ITALY

Born in Castiglione, diocese of Forlì-Bertinoro, March 21, 1922; ordained April 20, 1946; named titular Archbishop of Mauriana May 24, 1969; consecrated June 22, 1969; Pro-Prefect of the Congregation for Catholic Education (of Seminaries and of Institutes of Study), April 6, 1990; created and proclaimed a cardinal by John Paul II in the Consistory of June 28, 1991; given the titular church of S. Maria Ausiliatrice in Via Tuscolana; *Prefect emeritus* of the Congregation for Catholic Education; *Patron* of the Sovereign Military Order of Malta, May 8, 1993.

CASSIDY Edward Idris

AUSTRALIA

Born in Sydney July 5, 1924; ordained July 23, 1949; named titular Archbishop of Amanzia October 27, 1970; consecrated November 15, 1970; created and proclaimed a cardinal by John Paul II in the Consistory of June 28, 1991; given the titular church of S. Maria in Via Lata; *President emeritus* of the Pontifical Council for the Promotion of Christian Unity.

SÁNCHEZ José T.
PHILIPPINES

Born in Pandan, diocese of Virac, March 17, 1920; ordained May 12, 1946; named titular Bishop of Lesvi February 5, 1968; consecrated May 12, 1968; succeeded to the See of Lucena September 25, 1976; promoted to Nueva Segovia January 12, 1982; retired March 22, 1986; created and proclaimed a cardinal by John Paul II in the Consistory of June 28, 1991; given the titular church of S. Pio Va Villa Carpegna; *Prefect emeritus* of the Congregation for the Clergy.

NOÉ Virgilio
ITALY

Born in Zelata di Bereguardo, diocese of Pavia, March 30, 1922; ordained October 1, 1944; named titular Archbishop of Voncaria January 30, 1982; consecrated March 6, 1982; created and proclaimed a cardinal by John Paul II in the Consistory of June 28, 1991; given the titular church of S. Giovanni Bosco in Via Tuscolana; *Archpriest* of the Patriarchal Vatican Basilica; *Vicar General* of Vatican City State; *President* of the Fabric of St. Peter, July 1, 1991.

ANGELINI Fiorenzo
ITALY

Born in Rome August 1, 1916; ordained February 3, 1940; named titular Bishop of Messene June 27, 1956; consecrated July 29, 1956; promoted Archbishop February 11, 1985; created and proclaimed a cardinal by John Paul II in the Consistory of June 28, 1991; given the titular church of S. Spirito in Sassia; *President emeritus* of the Pontifical Council for the Pastoral Care of Health Workers.

SFEIR
Nasrallah Pierre
LEBANON

Born in Reyfoun, eparchy of Sarba dei Maroniti, May 15, 1920; ordained May 7, 1950; elected titular Bishop of Tarsus of the Maronites June 19 and confirmed June 23, 1962; consecrated July 16, 1961; named Patriarch of Antioch of the Maronites April 19, 1986.
The Holy Father granted him ecclesiastical communion May 7, 1986; created and proclaimed a cardinal by John Paul II in the Consistory of November 26, 1994; *Patriarch* of Antioch of the Maronites.

VLK Miloslav
CZECH REPUBLIC

Born in Lišnice-Sepekov May 17, 1932; ordained June 23, 1968; named Bishop of Ceské Budějovice February 14, 1990; consecrated March 31, 1990; promoted to Prague March 27, 1991; created and proclaimed a cardinal by John Paul II in the Consistory of November 26, 1994; given the titular church of S. Croce in Gerusalemme; *Archbishop* of Prague.

POGGI Luigi
ITALY

Born in Piacenza November 25, 1917; ordained July 28, 1940; named titular Archbishop of Forontoniana April 3, 1965; consecrated May 9, 1965; created and proclaimed a cardinal by John Paul II in the Consistory of November 26, 1994; given the titular church of S. Maria in Domnica; *Archivist* and *Librarian emeritus* of the Holy Roman Church.

SHIRAYANAGI Peter Seiichi
JAPAN

Born in Hachiōji, archdiocese of Tokyo, June 17, 1928; ordained December 21, 1954; named titular Bishop of Atenia March 15, 1966; consecrated May 8, 1966; promoted titular Archbishop of Castro November 15, 1969; succeeded to the see of Tokyo February 21, 1970; created and proclaimed a cardinal by John Paul II in the Consistory of November 26, 1994; given the titular church of S. Emerenziana a Tor Fiorenza; *Archbishop emeritus* of Tokyo (retired February 17, 2000).

FURNO Carlo
ITALY

Born in Bairo Canavese, diocese of Ivrea, December 2, 1921; ordained June 25, 1944; named titular Archbishop of Abari August 1, 1973; consecrated September 16, 1973; created and proclaimed a cardinal by John Paul II in the Consistory of November 26, 1994; given the titular church of S. Cuore di Cristo Re; *Grand Master* of the Equestrian Order of the Holy Sepulchre of Jerusalem December 16, 1995; *Archpriest* of the Patriarchal Basilica of Santa Maria Maggiore, September 29, 1997.

WINNING Thomas Joseph
GREAT BRITAIN

Born in Wishaw, diocese of Motherwell, June 3, 1925;
ordained December 18, 1948; named titular Bishop of Lugma
October 22, 1971; consecrated November 30, 1971;
promoted to Glasgow April 23, 1974; created and proclaimed
a cardinal by John Paul II in the Consistory of November 26,
1994; given the titular church of S. Andrea delle Fratte;
Archbishop of Glasgow.

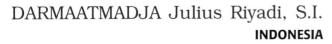

SUÁREZ RIVERA Adolfo Antonio
MEXICO

Born in San Cristóbal de las Casas January 9, 1927; ordained
March 8, 1952; named Bishop of Tepic May 14, 1971;
consecrated August 15, 1971; transferred to Tlalnepantla May 8,
1980; promoted to Monterrey November 8, 1983; created and
proclaimed a cardinal by John Paul II in the Consistory of
November 26, 1994; given the titular church of Nostra Signora di
Guadalupe a Monte Mario; *Archbishop* of Monterrey.

DARMAATMADJA Julius Riyadi, S.I.
INDONESIA

Born in Muntilan, archdiocese of Semarang, December 20, 1934;
ordained December 18, 1969; named Bishop of Semarang
February 19, 1983; consecrated June 29, 1983; created and
proclaimed a cardinal by John Paul II in the Consistory of
November 26, 1994; given the titular church of S. Cuore di Maria;
transferred to Jakarta January 11, 1996; *Archbishop* of Jakarta;
Military Ordinary for Indonesia.

ORTEGA Y ALAMINO Jaime Lucas
CUBA

Born in Jagüey Grande, diocese of Matanzas, October 18, 1936; ordained August 2, 1964; named Bishop of Pinar del Rio December 4, 1978; consecrated January 14, 1979; promoted to San Cristóbal de La Habana November 20, 1981; created and proclaimed a cardinal by John Paul II in the Consistory of November 26, 1994; given the titular church of Ss. Aquila e Priscilla; *Archbishop* of San Cristóbal de La Habana.

SCHOTTE Jan Pieter, C.I.C.M.
BELGIUM

Born in Beveren-Leie, diocese of Bruges, April 29, 1928; ordained August 3, 1952; named titular Bishop of Silli December 20, 1983; consecrated January 6, 1984; promoted Archbishop April 24, 1985; created and proclaimed a cardinal by John Paul II in the Consistory of November 26, 1994; given the titular church of S. Giuliana dei Fiamminghi; *Secretary General* of the Synod of Bishops, April 24, 1985; *President* of the Labour Office of the Apostolic See, April 14, 1989.

EYT Pierre
FRANCE

Born in Laruns, diocese of Bayonne, June 4, 1934; ordained June 29, 1961; named Coadjutor Bishop of Bordeaux June 7, 1986; consecrated September 28, 1986; succeeded to the see of Bordeaux May 31, 1989; created and proclaimed a cardinal by John Paul II in the Consistory of November 26, 1994; given the titular church of Ss. Trinità al Monte Pincio; *Archbishop* of Bordeaux.

AGUSTONI Gilberto
SWITZERLAND

Born in Schaffhausen, diocese of Basel, July 26, 1922; ordained April 20, 1946; named titular Bishop of Caorle December 18, 1986; consecrated January 6, 1987; created and proclaimed a cardinal by John Paul II in the Consistory of November 26, 1994; given the titular church of Ss. Urbano e Lorenzo a Prima Porta; *Prefect emeritus* of the Supreme Tribunal of the Apostolic Signature.

WAMALA Emmanuel
UGANDA

Born in Kamaggwa, diocese of Masaka, December 15, 1926; ordained December 21, 1957; named Bishop of Kiyinda-Mityana July 17, 1981; consecrated November 22, 1981; promoted Coadjutor Bishop of Kampala June 1988; succeeded to the see of Kampala February 8, 1990; created and proclaimed a cardinal by John Paul II in the Consistory of November 26, 1994; given the titular church of S. Ugo; *Archbishop* of Kampala.

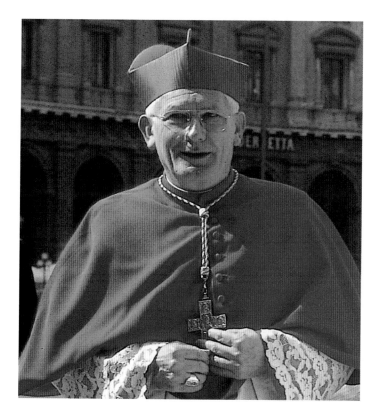

KEELER William Henry
UNITED STATES

Born in San Antonio March 4, 1931; ordained July 17, 1955; named titular Bishop of Dulcigno July 24, 1979; consecrated September 21, 1979; transferred to Harrisburg November 10, 1983; promoted to Baltimore April 6, 1989; created and proclaimed a cardinal by John Paul II in the Consistory of November 26, 1994; given the titular church of S. Maria degli Angeli; *Archbishop* of Baltimore.

TURCOTTE Jean-Claude
CANADA

Born in Montréal June 26, 1936; ordained May 24, 1959; named titular Bishop of Suas April 14, 1982; consecrated June 29, 1982; promoted to Montreal March 17, 1990; created and proclaimed a cardinal by John Paul II in the Consistory of November 26, 1994; given the titular church of Nostra Signora del Ss. Sacramento e Santi Martiri Canadesi; *Archbishop* of Montréal.

CARLES GORDÓ Ricardo María
SPAIN

Born in Valencia September 24, 1926; ordained June 29, 1951; named Bishop of Tortosa June 6, 1969; consecrated August 3, 1969; promoted to Barcelona March 23, 1990; created and proclaimed a cardinal by John Paul II in the Consistory of November 26, 1994; given the titular church of S. Maria Consolatrice al Tiburtino; *Archbishop* of Barcelona.

MAIDA Adam Joseph
UNITED STATES

Born in East Vandergrift, diocese of Greensburg, March 18, 1930; ordained May 26, 1956; named Bishop of Green Bay November 7, 1983; consecrated January 26, 1984; promoted to Detroit April 28, 1990; created and proclaimed a cardinal by John Paul II in the Consistory of November 26, 1994; given the titular church of Ss. Vitale, Valeria, Gervasio e Protasio; *Archbishop* of Detroit; *Superior* of the Cayman Islands.

PULJIĆ Vinko
BOSNIA - HERZEGOVINA

Born in Prijećani, diocese of Banja Luka, September 8, 1945; ordained June 29, 1970; named Bishop of Vrhbosna November 19, 1990; consecrated January 6, 1991; created and proclaimed a cardinal by John Paul II in the Consistory of November 26, 1994; given the titular church of S. Chiara a Vigna Clara; *Archbishop* of Vrhbosna.

RAZAFINDRATANDRA Armand Gaétan
MADAGASCAR

Born in Ambohimalaza, archdiocese of Antananarivo, August 7, 1925; ordained July 27, 1954; named Bishop of Mahajanga April 27, 1978; consecrated July 2, 1978; promoted to the see of Antananarivo February 3, 1994; created and proclaimed a cardinal by John Paul II in the Consistory of November 26, 1994; given the titular church of Ss. Silvestro e Martino ai Monti; *Archbishop* of Antananarivo.

PHAM ĐÌNH TUNG Paul Joseph
VIETNAM

Born in Binh Hoa, diocese of Phát Diêm, June 15, 1919; ordained June 6, 1949; named Bishop of Bac Ninh April 5, 1963; consecrated August 15, 1963; promoted to Hà Nôi March 23, 1994; created and proclaimed a cardinal by John Paul II in the Consistory of November 26, 1994; given the titular church of S. Maria Regina Pacis in Ostia mare; *Archbishop* of Hà Nôi.

SANDOVAL ÍÑIGUEZ Juan
MEXICO

Born in Yahualica, diocese of San Juan de los Lagos, March 28, 1933; ordained October 27, 1957; named Coadjutor of Ciudad Juárez March 3, 1988; consecrated April 30, 1988; became Bishop of Ciudad Juárez July 11, 1992; promoted to Guadalajara April 21, 1994; created and proclaimed a cardinal by John Paul II in the Consistory of November 26, 1994; given the titular church of Nostra Signora di Guadalupe e S. Filippo Martire in Via Aurelia; *Archbishop* of Guadalajara.

ŚWIĄTEK Kazimierz
BELARUS

Born in Walga, apostolic administration of Estonia, October 21, 1914; ordained April 8, 1939; named Bishop of Minsk-Mohilev April 13, 1991; consecrated May 21, 1991; created and proclaimed a cardinal by John Paul II in the Consistory of November 26, 1994; given the titular church of S. Gerardo Maiella; *Archbishop* of Minsk-Mohilev; *Apostolic Administrator* in the name of the Holy See to Pinsk.

TONINI Ersilio
ITALY

Born in Centovera di San Giorgio Piacentino, diocese of Piacenza Bobbio, July 20, 1914; ordained April 18, 1937; named Bishop of Macerata e Tolentino April 28, 1969; consecrated June 2, 1969; promoted to Ravenna e Cervia November 22, 1975; created and proclaimed a cardinal by John Paul II in the Consistory of November 26, 1994; given the titular church of Ss. Redentore in Val Melaina; *Archbishop emeritus* of Ravenna-Cervia (retired October 27, 1990).

MEDINA ESTÉVEZ
Jorge Arturo
CHILE

Born in Santiago del Cile December 23, 1926; ordained June 12, 1954; named titular Bishop of Tibili December 18, 1984; consecrated January 6, 1985; transferred to Rancagua November 25, 1987; transferred to Valparaiso April 16, 1993 (retired June 21, 1996); promoted to Archbishop September 19, 1996; created and proclaimed a cardinal by John Paul II in the Consistory of February 21, 1988; given the titular church of S. Saba; *Prefect* of the Congregation for Divine Worship and the Discipline of the Sacraments.

CASTRILLÓN HOYOS Darío
COLOMBIA

Born in Medellín July 4, 1929; ordained October 26, 1952; named titular Bishop of Villa del Re June 2, 1971; consecrated July 18, 1971; succeeded to the see of Pereira July 1, 1976; promoted to Bucaramanga December 16, 1992 (retired June 15, 1996); created and proclaimed a cardinal by John Paul II in the Consistory of February 21, 1988; given the titular church of Ss. Nome di Maria al Foro Triano; *Prefect* of the Congregation for the Clergy, February 23, 1998; *President* of the Pontifical Commission "Ecclesia Dei," April 13, 2000.

ANTONETTI Lorenzo

ITALY

Born in Romagnano Sesia, diocese of Novara, July 31, 1922; ordained May 26, 1945; named titular Archbishop of Roselle February 23, 1968; consecrated May 12, 1968; created and proclaimed a cardinal by John Paul II in the Consistory of February 21, 1988; given the titular church of S. Agnese in Agone; *President emeritus* of the Administration of the Patrimony of the Holy See; *Pontifical Delegate* of the Patriarchal Basilica of S. Francisco in Assisi, November 5, 1998.

STAFFORD James Francis

UNITED STATES

Born in Baltimore July 26, 1932; ordained December 15, 1957; named titular Bishop of Respetta January 19, 1976; consecrated February 29, 1976; transferred to Memphis November 17, 1982; promoted to Denver May 30, 1986 (retired August 20, 1996); created and proclaimed a cardinal by John Paul II in the Consistory of February 21, 1988; given the titular church of Gesu Buon Pastore alla Montagnola; *President* of the Pontifical Council for the Laity, August 20, 1996.

DE GIORGI Salvatore

ITALY

Born in Vernole, archdiocese of Lecce, September 6, 1930; ordained June 28, 1953; named titular Bishop of Tulana November 21, 1973; consecrated December 27, 1973; succeeded to the see of Oria March 17, 1978; promoted to Foggia and nominated to Bovino and to Troia April 4, 1981; transferred to Taranto October 1987(retired May 11, 1990); transferred to Palermo April 4, 1996; created and proclaimed a cardinal by John Paul II in the Consistory of February 21, 1988; given the titular church of S. Maria in Ara Coeli; *Archbishop* of Palermo.

de ARAÚJO FERNANDES Serafim
BRAZIL

Born in Minas Novas, diocese of Araçuaí, August 13, 1924; ordained March 12, 1949; named titular Bishop of Verinopoli January 19, 1959; consecrated May 7, 1959; promoted Coadjutor of Belo Horizonte November 22, 1982; succeeded to the see of Belo Horizonte February 5, 1986; created and proclaimed a cardinal by John Paul II in the Consistory of February 21, 1988; given the titular church of S. Luigi Maria Grignion de Montfort; *Archbishop* of Belo Horizonte.

ROUCO VARELA Antonio María
SPAIN

Born in Villalba, diocese of Mondoñedo-Ferrol, August 24, 1936; ordained March 28, 1959; named titular Bishop of Gergi September 17, 1976; consecrated October 31, 1976; promoted to Santiago de Compostela May 9, 1984; transferred to Madrid July 28, 1994; created and proclaimed a cardinal by John Paul II in the Consistory of February 21, 1988; given the titular church of S. Lorenzo in Damasco; *Archbishop* of Madrid.

AMBROZIC Aloysius Matthew
CANADA

Born in Gabrje, archdiocese of Ljubljana, January 27, 1930; ordained June 4, 1955; named Bishop of Valabria March 26, 1976; consecrated May 27, 1976; promoted Coadjutor of Toronto May 22, 1986; succeeded to the see of Toronto March 17, 1990; created and proclaimed a cardinal by John Paul II in the Consistory of February 21, 1988; given the titular church of Ss. Marcellino e Pietro; *Archbishop* of Toronto.

TETTAMANZI Dionigi
ITALY

Born in Renate, archdiocese of Milan, March 14, 1934; ordained June 28, 1957; named Bishop of Ancona-Osimo July 1, 1989; consecrated September 23, 1989; retired April 6, 1991; transferred to Genova April 20, 1995; created and proclaimed a cardinal by John Paul II in the Consistory of February 21, 1988; given the titular church of Ss. Ambrogio e Carlo; *Archbishop* of Genova.

PENGO Polycarp
TANZANIA

Born in Mwazye, diocese of Sumbawanga, August 5, 1944; ordained June 20, 1971; named Bishop of Nachingwea November 11, 1983; consecrated January 6, 1984; transferred to Tunduro-Masasi October 17, 1986; promoted Coadjutor of Dar-es-Salaam January 22, 1990; succeeded to the see of Dar-es-Salaam July 22, 1992; created and proclaimed a cardinal by John Paul II in the Consistory of February 21, 1988; given the titular church of Nostra Signora de La Salette; *Archbishop* of Dar-es-Salaam.

SCHÖNBORN Christoph, O.P.
AUSTRIA

Born in Skalsko, diocese of Litoměřice, January 22, 1945; ordained December 27, 1970; named Bishop of Sutri July 11, 1991; consecrated September 29, 1991; promoted Coadjutor of Vienna April 13, 1995; succeeded to the see of Vienna September 14, 1995; created and proclaimed a cardinal by John Paul II in the Consistory of February 21, 1998; given the titular church of Gesù Divin Lavoratore; *Archbishop* of Vienna; *Ordinary* for the eastern rite faithful in Austria in absence of a local Ordinary.

RIVERA CARRERA Norberto
MEXICO

Born in Tepehuanes, archdiocese of Durango, June 6, 1942; ordained July 3, 1966; named Bishop of Tehuacan November 5, 1985; consecrated December 21, 1985; promoted to Mexico City June 13, 1995; created and proclaimed a cardinal by John Paul II in the Consistory of February 21, 1988; given the titular church of S. Francesco d'Assisi a Ripa Grande; *Archbishop* of Mexico City.

GEORGE Francis Eugene, O.M.I.
UNITED STATES

Born in Chicago January 16, 1937; ordained December 21, 1965; named Bishop of Yakima July 10, 1990; consecrated September 21, 1990; promoted to Portland April 30, 1996; transferred to Chicago April 8, 1997; created and proclaimed a cardinal by John Paul II in the Consistory of February 21, 1988; given the titular church of S. Bartolomeo all'Isola; *Archbishop* of Chicago.

SHAN KUO-HSI Paul, S.I.
TAIWAN

Born in Puyang, diocese of Taming, December 3, 1923; ordained March 18, 1955; named Bishop of Hwalien November 15, 1979; consecrated February 14, 1980; transferred to Kaohsiung March 4, 1991; created and proclaimed a cardinal by John Paul II in the Consistory of February 21, 1988; given the titular church of S. Crisogono; *Bishop* of Kaohsiung.

KOZŁOWIECKI Adam, S.I.

POLAND

Born in Huta Komorowaska, diocese of Sandomierz, April 1, 1911; ordained June 24, 1937; named Bishop of Diospoli inferiore June 4, 1955; consecrated September 11, 1955; promoted to Lusaka April 25, 1959; transferred to Potenza Picena with the personal title of Archbishop May 29, 1969; created and proclaimed a cardinal by John Paul II in the Consistory of February 21, 1988; given the titular church of S. Andrea al Quirinale.

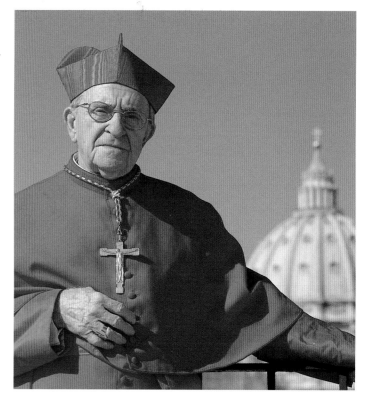

CHELI Giovanni

ITALY

Born in Turin October 4, 1918; ordained June 21, 1942; named titular Archbishop of Santa Giusta September 8, 1978; consecrated September 16, 1978; created and proclaimed a cardinal by John Paul II in the Consistory of February 21, 1988; given the titular church of Ss. Cosma e Damiano; *President Emeritus* of the Pontifical Council for the Pastoral Care of Migrants and Itinerant Workers.

COLASUONNO Francesco

ITALY

Born in Gruma Appula, archdiocese of Bari-Bitonto, January 2, 1925; ordained September 28, 1947; named titular Archbishop of Tronto December 6, 1974; consecrated February 9, 1975; created and proclaimed a cardinal by John Paul II in the Consistory of February 21, 1988; given the titular church of S. Eugenio.

MONDUZZI Dino
ITALY

Born in Brisighella, diocese of Faenza-Modigliana, April 2, 1922; ordained July 22, 1945; named Bishop of Capri December 18, 1986; consecrated January 6, 1987; created and proclaimed a cardinal by John Paul II in the Consistory of February 21, 1988; given the titular church of S. Sebastiano al Palatino; *Prefect emeritus* of the Papal Household.

JAWORSKI Marian
UKRAINE

Born in Lviv August 21, 1926; ordained June 25, 1950; named titular Bishop of Lambesi May 21, 1984; consecrated June 23, 1984; promoted to Lviv dei Latini January 16, 1991; created and proclaimed a cardinal by John Paul II in the Consistory of February 21, 1988; given the titular church of S. Sisto; *Archbishop* of Lviv dei Latini.

PUJATS Jānis
LATVIA

Born in Nautreni, archdiocese of Riga, November 14, 1930; ordained March 29, 1951; named Bishop of Riga May 8, 1991; consecrated June 1, 1991; created and proclaimed a cardinal by John Paul II in the Consistory of February 21, 1988; given the titular church of S. Silvia; *Archbishop* of Riga.

RE Giovanni Battista

ITALY

Born in Borno, diocese of Brescia, January 30, 1934; ordained March 3, 1957; named titular Archbishop of Vescovío October 9, 1987; consecrated November 7, 1987; created and proclaimed a cardinal by John Paul II in the Consistory of February 21, 2001; given the titular church of Ss. XII Apostoli; *Prefect* of the Congregation for Bishops; *President* of the Pontifical Commission for Latin America, September 16, 2000.

NGUYÊN VAN THUÂN
François Xavier

VIETNAM

Born in Huê April 17, 1928; ordained June 11, 1953; named Bishop of Nha Trang April 13, 1967; consecrated June 24, 1967; named titular Archbishop of Vadesi April 24, 1975, Coadjutor Bishop of Thành-Phô Hô Chi Minh (retired November 24, 1994); created and proclaimed a cardinal by John Paul II in the Consistory of February 21, 2001; given the titular church of S. Maria della Scala; *President* of the Pontifical Council for Justice and Peace, June 24, 1998.

CACCIAVILLAN
Agostino
ITALY

Born in Novale, diocese of Vicenza, August 14, 1926; ordained June 26, 1949; named titular Archbishop of Amiterno January 17, 1976; consecrated February 28, 1976; created and proclaimed a cardinal by John Paul II in the Consistory of February 21, 2001; given the titular church of Ss. Angeli Custodi a Città Giardino; *President* of the Administration of the Patrimony of the Apostolic See.

SEBASTIANI Sergio
ITALY

Born in Montemonaco, diocese of San Benedetto del Tronto-Ripatransone-Montalto, April 11, 1931; ordained July 15, 1956; named titular Archbishop of Cesarea di Mauritania September 27, 1976; consecrated October 30, 1976; created and proclaimed a cardinal by John Paul II in the Consistory of February 21, 2001; given the titular church of S. Eustachio; *President* of the Prefecture for the Economic Affairs of the Holy See, November 3, 1997.

GROCHOLEWSKI
Zenon
POLAND

Born in Bródki, archdiocese of Poznań, October 11, 1939; ordained May 27, 1963, named titular Bishop of Agropoli December 21, 1982; consecrated January 6, 1983, promoted Archbishop December 16, 1991; created and proclaimed a cardinal by John Paul II in the Consistory of February 21, 2001; given the titular church of S. Nicola in Carcere; *Prefect* of the Congregation for Catholic Education, November 15, 1999.

SARAIVA MARTINS
José, C.M.F.
PORTUGAL

Born in Gagos, diocese of Guarda, January 6, 1932; ordained March 16, 1957; named titular Archbishop of Tuburnica May 26, 1988; consecrated July 2, 1988; created and proclaimed a cardinal by John Paul II in the Consistory of February 21, 2001; given the titular church of Nostra Signora del S. Cuore; *Prefect* of the Congregation for the Causes of Saints, May 30, 1998.

SEPE Crescenzio
ITALY

Born in Carinaro, diocese of Aversa, June 2, 1943; ordained March 12, 1967; named titular Archbishop of Grado April 2, 1992; consecrated April 26, 1992; created and proclaimed a cardinal by John Paul II in the Consistory of February 21, 2001; given the titular church of Dio Padre Misericordioso; *President* of the "Peregrinatio ad Petri Sedem", November 8, 1997; *Prefect* of the Congregation for the Evangelization of Peoples, April 9, 2001.

MEJÍA Jorge María
ARGENTINA

Born in Buenos Aires January 31, 1923; ordained September 22, 1945; named titular Bishop of Apollonia March 8, 1986; consecrated April 12, 1986; named Archbishop March 5, 1994; created and proclaimed a cardinal by John Paul II in the Consistory of February 21, 2001; given the titular church of S. Girolamo della Carità; *Archivist* and *Librarian* of the Holy Roman Church, March 7, 1998.

DAOUD
Ignace Moussa I
SYRIA

Born in Meskané, archparish of Homs dei Siri, September 18, 1930; ordained October 17, 1954; elected Bishop of Le Caire dei Siri July 2 , 1977; consecrated September 18, 1977; promoted to Homs dei Siri July 1, 1994; elected Patriarch of Antioch of the Syrians October 13, 1998. The Holy Father granted him "ecclesiastical communion" October 20, 1998; created and proclaimed a cardinal by John Paul II in the Consistory of February 21, 2001; *Patriarch emeritus* of Antioch of the Syrians (retired January 8, 2001); *Prefect* of the Congregation for Oriental Churches, November 25, 2000.

141

POMPEDDA Mario Francesco
ITALY

Born in Ozieri April 18, 1929; ordained December 23, 1951; named titular Archbishop of Bisarcio November 29, 1997; consecrated January 6, 1998; created and proclaimed a cardinal by John Paul II in the Consistory of February 21, 2001; given the titular church of Annunciazione della B.V.M. a Via Ardeatina; *Prefect* of the Supreme Tribunal of the Apostolic Signature, November 16, 1999.

KASPER Walter
GERMANY

Born in Heidenheim/Brenz, diocese of Rottenburg-Stuttgart, March 5, 1933; ordained April 6, 1957; named Bishop of Rottenburg-Stuttgart April 17, 1989; consecrated June 17, 1989; retired May 31, 1999; created and proclaimed a cardinal by John Paul II in the Consistory of February 21, 2001; given the titular church of Ognissanti in Via Appia Nuova; *President* of the Pontifical Council for the Promotion of Christian Unity, March 3, 2001.

DEGENHARDT Johannes Joachim
GERMANY

Born in Schwelm, diocese of Essen, January 31, 1926; ordained August 6, 1952; named titular Bishop of Vico di Pacato March 12, 1968; consecrated May 1, 1968; promoted to Paderborn April 4, 1974; consecrated January 6, 1998; created and proclaimed a cardinal by John Paul II in the Consistory of February 21, 2001; given the titular church of S. Liborio; *Archbishop* of Paderborn.

GONZÁLEZ ZUMÁRRAGA Antonio José
ECUADOR

Born in Pujilí, diocese of Latacunga, March 18, 1925; ordained June 29, 1951; named titular Bishop of Tagarata May 17, 1969; consecrated June 15, 1969; transferred to Machala January 30, 1978; promoted Coadjutor of Quito June 28, 1980; named Bishop of Quito June 1, 1985; consecrated January 6, 1998; created and proclaimed a cardinal by John Paul II in the Consistory of February 21, 2001; given the titular church of S. Maria in Via; *Archbishop* of Quito.

DIAS Ivan
INDIA

Born in Mumbai April 14, 1936; ordained December 8, 1958; named titular Archbishop of Rusubisir May 8, 1982; consecrated June 19, 1982; transferred to Bombay November 8, 1996; consecrated January 6, 1998; created and proclaimed a cardinal by John Paul II in the Consistory of February 21, 2001; given the titular church of Spirito Santo alla Ferratella; *Archbishop* of Bombay.

AGNELO Geraldo Majella
BRAZIL

Born in Juiz de Fora October 19, 1933; ordained June 29, 1957; named Bishop of Toledo May 5, 1978; consecrated August 6, 1978; promoted to Londrina October 4, 1982; retired September 16, 1991; transferred to São Salvador da Bahia January 13, 1999; consecrated January 6, 1998; created and proclaimed a cardinal by John Paul II in the Consistory of February 21, 2001; given the titular church of S. Gregorio Magno alla Magliana Nuova; *Archbishop* of São Salvador da Bahia

RUBIANO SÁENZ Pedro
COLOMBIA

Born in Cartago September 13, 1932; ordained July 8, 1956; named Bishop of Cúcuta June 2, 1971; consecrated July 11, 1971; named Coadjutor Bishop of Cali March 26, 1983; succeeded to the see of Cali February 7, 1985; transferred to Bogotá December 27, 1994; created and proclaimed a cardinal by John Paul II in the Consistory of February 21, 2001; given the titular church of the Trasfigurazione di Nostro Signore Gesù Cristo; *Archbishop* of Bogotá.

McCARRICK Theodore Edgar
UNITED STATES

Born in New York July 7, 1930; ordained May 31, 1956; named Bishop of Rusubisir May 24, 1977; consecrated June 29, 1977; transferred to Metuchen November 19, 1981; promoted to Newark May 30, 1986; transferred to Washington November 21, 2000; created and proclaimed a cardinal by John Paul II in the Consistory of February 21, 2001; given the titular church of Ss. Nereo e Achilleo; *Archbishop* of Washington.

CONNELL Desmond

IRELAND

Born in Dublin March 24, 1926; ordained May 19, 1951; named Bishop of Dublin January 21, 1988; consecrated March 6, 1988; created and proclaimed a cardinal by John Paul II in the Consistory of February 21, 2001; given the titular church of S. Silvestro in Capite; *Archbishop* of Dublin.

BAČKIS Audrys Juozas

LITHUANIA

Born in Kaunas February 1, 1937; ordained March 18, 1961; named titular Archbishop of Meta August 5, 1988; consecrated October 4, 1988; transferred to Vilnius December 24, 1991; created and proclaimed a cardinal by John Paul II in the Consistory of February 21, 2001; given the titular church of the Natività di Nostro Signore Gesù Cristo in Via Gallia; *Archbishop* of Vilnius.

ERRÁZURIZ OSSA Francisco Javier

CHILE

Born in Santiago del Cile September 5, 1933; ordained July 16, 1961; named titular Archbishop of Hólar December 22, 1990; consecrated January 6, 1991; transferred to Valparaíso September 24, 1996; transferred to Santiago del Cile April 24, 1998; created and proclaimed a cardinal by John Paul II in the Consistory of February 21, 2001; given the titular church of S. Maria della Pace; *Archbishop* of Santiago del Cile.

TERRAZAS SANDOVAL
Julio, C.SS.R.
BOLIVIA

Born a Vallegrande, archdiocese of Santa Cruz de la Sierra, March 7, 1936; ordained July 29, 1962; named titular Archbishop of Apisa maggiore April 15, 1978; consecrated June 8, 1978; transferred to Oruro January 9; 1982; promoted to Santa Cruz de la Sierra February 6, 1991; created and proclaimed a cardinal by John Paul II in the Consistory of February 21, 2001; given the titular church of S. Giovanni Battista de' Rossi; *Archbishop* of Santa Cruz de la Sierra.

NAPIER Wilfrid Fox, O.F.M.
SOUTH AFRICA

Born in Swartberg, diocese of Kokstad, March 8, 1941; ordained July 25, 1970; named Bishop of Kokstad November 29, 1980; consecrated February 28, 1981; promoted to Durban May 29, 1992; created and proclaimed a cardinal by John Paul II in the Consistory of February 21, 2001; given the titular church of S. Francesco d'Assisi ad Acilia; *Archbishop* of Durban; *Apostolic Administrator* "sede vacante et ad nutum Sanctae Sedis" of Umzimkulu.

RODRÍGUEZ MARADIAGA
Oscar Andrés, S.D.B.
HONDURAS

Born in Tegucigalpa Dember 29, 1942; ordained June 28, 1970; named titular Bishop of Pudenziana October 28, 1978; consecrated December 8, 1978; promoted to Tegucigalpa January 8, 1993; created and proclaimed a cardinal by John Paul II in the Consistory of February 21, 2001; given the titular church of S. Maria della Speranza; *Archbishop* of Tegucigalpa.

AGRÉ Bernard
IVORY COAST

Born in Monga, archdiocese of Abidjan, March 2, 1926; ordained July 20, 1953; named Bishop of Man June 8, 1968; consecrated October 3, 1968; transferred to Yamoussoukro March 6, 1992; promoted to Abidjan December 19, 1994; created and proclaimed a cardinal by John Paul II in the Consistory of February 21, 2001; given the titular church of S. Giovanni Crisostomo a Monte Sacro Alto; *Archbishop* of Abidjan.

BILLÉ Louis-Marie
FRANCE

Born in Fleury-lès-Aubrais, diocese of Orleans, February 18, 1938; ordained March 25, 1962; named Bishop of Laval March 10, 1984; consecrated May 19, 1984; promoted to Aix May 5, 1995; transferred to Lyon July 10, 1998; created and proclaimed a cardinal by John Paul II in the Consistory of February 21, 2001; given the titular church of S. Pietro in Vincoli; *Archbishop* of Lyon.

VELASCO GARCÍA Ignacio Antonio, S.D.B.
VENEZUELA

Born in Acarigua, diocese of Guanare, January 17, 1929; ordained December 17, 1955; named titular Bishop of Utimmira October 23, 1989; consecrated January 6, 1990; promoted to Caracas May 27, 1995; created and proclaimed a cardinal by John Paul II in the Consistory of February 21, 2001; given the titular church of S. Maria Domenica Mazzarello; *Archbishop* of Caeacas.

CIPRIANI THORNE Juan Luis
PERÚ

A priest of the personal Prelature of Opus Dei, born in Lima December 28, 1943; ordained August 21, 1977; named titular Bishop of Turuzi May 23, 1988; consecrated July 3, 1988; promoted to Ayacucho May 13, 1995; transferred to Lima January 9, 1990; created and proclaimed a cardinal by John Paul II in the Consistory of February 21, 2001; given the titular church of S. Camillo de Lellis; *Archbishop* of Lima.

ÁLVAREZ MARTÍNEZ Francisco

SPAIN

Born in Santa Eulalia de Ferroñes Llanera, archdiocese of Oviedo, July 14, 1925; ordained June 11, 1950; named Bishop of Tarazona April 13, 1973; consecrated June 3, 1973; transferred to Calahorra y La Calzada-Logroño December 20, 1976; transferred to Orihuela - Alicante May 12, 1989; promoted to Toledo June 23, 1995; created and proclaimed a cardinal by John Paul II in the Consistory of February 21, 2001; given the titular church of S. Maria "Regina Pacis" a Monte Verde; *Archbishop* of Toledo.

HUMMES Cláudio, O.F.M.

BRAZIL

Born in Montenegro, archdiocese of Porto Alegre, August 8, 1934; ordained August 3, 1958; named titular Bishop of Carcabia March 22, 1975; consecrated May 25, 1975; succeeded to the see of Santo André December 29, 1975; promoted to Fortaleza May 29, 1996; transferred to São Paulo April 15, 1998; created and proclaimed a cardinal by John Paul II in the Consistory of February 21, 2001; given the titular church of S. Antonio da Padova in Via Merulana; *Archbishop* of São Paulo.

VITHAYATHIL Varkey, C.SS.R.

INDIA

Born in Parur, archparish of Ernakula-Angamaly of the Syro-Malabars, May 29, 1927; ordained June 12, 1954, named titular Archbishop of Acrida November 11, 1996; consecrated January 6, 1997; transferred to titular see of Antinoe April 19, 1997; promoted to Archbishop Major of Ernakulam-Angamaly of the Syro-Malabars December 18, 1999; created and proclaimed a cardinal by John Paul II in the Consistory of February 21, 2001; given the titular church of S. Bernardo alle Terme; *Archbishop Major* of Ernakulam-Angamaly of the Syro-Malabars.

BERGOGLIO Jorge Mario, S.I.

ARGENTINA

Born in Buenos Aires December 17, 1936; ordained December 13, 1969; named titular Bishop of Auca May 20, 1992; consecrated June 27, 1992; promoted Coadjutor of Buenos Aires June 3, 1997; succeeded to the see of Buenos Aires February 28, 1998; created and proclaimed a cardinal by John Paul II in the Consistory of February 21, 2001; given the titular church of S. Roberto Bellarmino; *Archbishop* of Buenos Aires; *Ordinary* for the eastern rite faithful in Argentina in absence of a local Ordinary.

da CRUZ POLICARPO José

PORTUGAL

Born in Alvorninha, Patriarchate of Lisbon, February 26, 1936; ordained August 15, 1961; named titular bishop of Caliabria May 26, 1978; consecrated June 29, 1978; promoted Coadjutor of Lisbon March 5, 1997; succeeded to the see of Lisbon March 24, 1998; created and proclaimed a cardinal by John Paul II in the Consistory of February 21, 2001; given the titular church of S. Antonio in Campo Marzio; *Patriarch* of Lisbon.

POLETTO Severino

ITALY

Born in Salgareda, diocese of Treviso, March 18, 1933; ordained June 29, 1957; named Coadjutor of Fossano April 3, 1980; consecrated May 17, 1980; succeeded to the see of Fossano October 29, 1980; transferred to Asti March 16, 1989; promoted to Turin June 19, 1999; created and proclaimed a cardinal by John Paul II in the Consistory of February 21, 2001; given the titular church of S. Giuseppe in Via Trionfale; *Archbishop* of Turin.

MURPHY-O'CONNOR Cormac

GREAT BRITAIN

Born in Reading, diocese of Portsmouth, August 24, 1932; ordained October 28, 1958; named Bishop of Arundel and Brighton November 17, 1977; consecrated December 21, 1977; promoted to Westminster February 15, 2000; created and proclaimed a cardinal by John Paul II in the Consistory of February 21, 2001; given the titular church of S. Maria sopra Minerva; *Archbishop* of Westminster.

EGAN Edward Michael

UNITED STATES

Born in Oak Park, archdiocese of Chicago, April 2, 1932; ordained December 15, 1957; named titular Bishop of Allegheny April 1, 1985; consecrated May 22, 1985; transferred to Bridgeport November 5, 1988; promoted to New York May 11, 2000; created and proclaimed a cardinal by John Paul II in the Consistory of February 21, 2001; given the titular church of Ss. Giovanni e Paolo; *Archbishop* of New York.

HUSAR Lubomyr

UKRAINE

Born in Lviv February 26, 1933; ordained March 30, 1958; consecrated April 2, 1977; confirmed and nominated to the titular see of Nisa di Licia February 22, 1996; promoted to Lviv January 25, 2001; created and proclaimed a cardinal by John Paul II in the Consistory of February 21, 2001; given the titular church of S. Sofia in Via Boccea; *Archbishop Major* of the Ukrainians of Lviv.

LEHMANN Karl
GERMANY

Born in Sigmaringen, archdiocese of Freiburg im Breisgau, May 16, 1936; ordained October 10, 1963; named Bishop of Mainz June 21, 1983; consecrated October 2, 1983; created and proclaimed a cardinal by John Paul II in the Consistory of February 21, 2001; given the titular church of S. Leone I; *Bishop* of Mainz.

GHATTAS Stéphanos II, C.M.
EGYPT

Born in Cheikh Zein-el-Dine, eparchy of Sohag of the Copts, January 16, 1920; ordained March 25, 1944; elected Bishop of Luxor of the Copts May 8, 1967; consecrated June 9, 1967; elected Patriarch of Alexandria of the Copts June 9, 1986. The Holy Father granted him "ecclesiastical communion" June 23, 1986; created and proclaimed a cardinal by John Paul II in the Consistory of February 21, 2001; *Patriarch* of Alexandria of the Copts.

HONORÉ Jean
FRANCE

Born in Saint-Brice-en-Coglès, archdiocese of Rennes, August 13, 1920; ordained June 29, 1943; named Bishop of Evreux October 24, 1972; consecrated December 17, 1972; promoted to Tours August 13, 1981; *Archbishop emeritus* of Tours (retired July 22, 1997); created and proclaimed a cardinal by John Paul II in the Consistory of February 21, 2001; given the titular church of S. Maria della Salute a Primavalle.

TUCCI Roberto, S.I.
ITALY

Born in Naples April 19, 1921; ordained August 24, 1950; created and proclaimed a cardinal by John Paul II in the Consistory of February 21, 2001; given the titular church of S. Ignazio di Loyola a Campo Marzio.

SCHEFFCZYK Leo
GERMANY

Born in Beuthen, archdiocese of Breslau, February 21, 1920; ordained June 29, 1947; created and proclaimed a cardinal by John Paul II in the Consistory of February 21, 2001; given the titular church of S. Francesco Savero alla Garbatella.

DULLES Avery, S.I.
UNITED STATES

Born in Auburn, diocese of Rochester, August 24, 1918; ordained June 16, 1956; created and proclaimed a cardinal by John Paul II in the Consistory of February 21, 2001; given the titular church of SS. Nomi di Gesù e Maria in Via Lata.

LIST OF CARDINALS DIVIDED BY NATIONALITY AND IN ORDER OF AGE

EUROPE

ITALY
BAFILE Corrado ----------------------------------- 04.07.1903
SENSI Giuseppe Maria ------------------------- 27.05.1907
BERTOLI Paolo ----------------------------------- 01.02.1908
URSI Corrado ------------------------------------- 26.07.1908
ROSSI Opilio -------------------------------------- 14.05.1910
ODDI Silvio -- 14.11.1910
SABATTANI Aurelio ------------------------------ 18.10.1912
TONINI Ersilio ------------------------------------ 20.07.1914
CAPRIO Giuseppe -------------------------------- 15.11.1914
INNOCENTI Antonio ----------------------------- 23.08.1915
ANGELINI Fiorenzo ------------------------------ 01.08.1916
POGGI Luigi --------------------------------------- 25.11.1917
PAPPALARDO Salvatore ------------------------- 23.09.1918
CANESTRI Giovanni ------------------------------ 30.09.1918
CHELI Giovanni ----------------------------------- 04.10.1918
FELICI Angelo ------------------------------------ 26.07.1919
TUCCI Roberto, S.I. ---------------------------- 19.04.1921
FURNO Carlo -------------------------------------- 02.12.1921
NOÉ Virgilio -------------------------------------- 30.03.1922
MONDUZZI Dino ---------------------------------- 02.04.1922
LAGHI Pio --- 21.05.1922
ANTONETTI Lorenzo ----------------------------- 31.07.1922
SILVESTRINI Achille ----------------------------- 25.10.1923
PIOVANELLI Silvano ----------------------------- 21.02.1924
SALDARINI Giovanni ----------------------------- 11.12.1924
COLASUONNO Francesco ----------------------- 02.01.1925
CÉ Marco -- 08.07.1925
CACCIAVILLAN Agostino ------------------------ 14.08.1926
MARTINI Carlo Maria, S.I. --------------------- 15.02.1927
SODANO Angelo ---------------------------------- 23.11.1927
BIFFI Giacomo ----------------------------------- 13.06.1928
POMPEDDA Mario Francesco ------------------ 18.04.1929
DE GIORGI Salvatore --------------------------- 06.09.1930
GIORDANO Michele ------------------------------ 26.09.1930
RUINI Camillo ------------------------------------ 19.02.1931
SEBASTIANI Sergio ------------------------------ 11.04.1931
POLETTO Severino ------------------------------- 18.03.1933
RE Giovanni Battista ---------------------------- 30.01.1934
TETTAMANZI Dionigi ---------------------------- 14.03.1934
SEPE Crescenzio --------------------------------- 02.06.1943

GERMANY
MAYER Paul Augustin, O.S.B. ------------------ 23.05.1911
SCHEFFCZYK Leo --------------------------------- 21.02.1920
DEGENHARDT Johannes Joachim ------------- 31.01.1926
RATZINGER Joseph ------------------------------ 16.04.1927
WETTER Friedrich -------------------------------- 20.02.1928
KASPER Walter ----------------------------------- 05.03.1933
MEISNER Joachim -------------------------------- 25.12.1933
STERZINSKY Georg Maximilian ---------------- 09.02.1936
LEHMANN Karl ------------------------------------ 16.05.1936

SPAIN
SUQUÍA GOICOECHEA Angel -------------------- 02.10.1916
GONZÁLEZ MARTÍN Marcelo ------------------- 16.01.1918
JAVIERRE ORTAS Antonio María, S.D.B. ---- 21.02.1921
ÁLVAREZ MARTÍNEZ Francisco ---------------- 14.07.1925
CARLES GORDÓ Ricardo María ---------------- 24.09.1926
MARTÍNEZ SOMALO Eduardo ------------------ 31.03.1927
ROUCO VARELA Antonio María ---------------- 24.08.1936

POLAND
KOZŁOWIECKI Adam, S.I. ---------------------- 01.04.1911
DESKUR Andrzej Maria -------------------------- 29.02.1924
MACHARSKI Franciszek ------------------------- 20.05.1927
GULBINOWICZ Henryk Roman ----------------- 17.10.1928
GLEMP Józef -------------------------------------- 18.12.1929

GROCHOLEWSKI Zenon -------------------------- 11.10.1939

FRANCE
HONORÉ Jean -------------------------------------- 13.08.1920
ETCHEGARAY Roger ------------------------------- 25.09.1922
LUSTIGER Jean-Marie ---------------------------- 17.09.1926
POUPARD Paul ------------------------------------- 30.08.1930
EYT Pierre --- 04.06.1934
BILLÉ Louis-Marie -------------------------------- 18.02.1938

AUSTRIA
KÖNIG Franz --------------------------------------- 03.08.1905
STICKLER Alfons Maria, S.D.B. ---------------- 23.08.1910
GROËR Hans Hermann, O.S.B. ----------------- 13.10.1919
SCHÖNBORN Christoph, O.P. -------------------- 22.01.1945

BELGIUM
SCHOTTE Jan Pieter, C.I.C.M. ------------------ 29.04.1928
DANNEELS Godfried ------------------------------ 04.06.1933

SLOVAKIA
KOREC Ján Chryzostom, S.I. ------------------- 22.01.1924
TOMKO Jozef -------------------------------------- 11.03.1924

SWITZERLAND
AGUSTONI Gilberto ------------------------------- 26.07.1922
SCHWERY Henri ----------------------------------- 14.06.1932

GREAT BRITAIN
WINNING Thomas Joseph ----------------------- 03.06.1925
MURPHY-O'CONNOR Cormac -------------------- 24.08.1932

PORTUGAL
SARAIVA MARTINS José, C.M.F. ---------------- 06.01.1932
da CRUZ POLICARPO José --------------------- 26.02.1936

UKRAINE
JAWORSKI Marian --------------------------------- 21.08.1926
HUSAR Lubomyr ----------------------------------- 26.02.1933

THE NETHERLANDS
WILLEBRANDS Johannes ------------------------- 04.09.1909
SIMONIS Adrianus Johannes -------------------- 26.11.1931

IRELAND
DALY Cahal Brendan ----------------------------- 01.10.1917
CONNELL Desmond -------------------------------- 24.03.1926

CZECH REPUBLIC
VLK Miloslav --------------------------------------- 17.05.1932

BOSNIA-HERZEGOVINA
PULJIĆ Vinko -------------------------------------- 08.09.1945

HUNGARY
PASKAI László, O.F.M. --------------------------- 08.05.1927

LITHUANIA
BAČKIS Audrys Juozas --------------------------- 01.02.1937

LATVIA
PUJATS Jānis -------------------------------------- 14.11.1930

CROATIA
KUHARIĆ Franjo ----------------------------------- 15.04.1919

ROMANIA
TODEA Alexandru --------------------------------- 05.06.1912

BELARUS
ŚWIĄTEK Kazimierz ------------------------------- 21.10.1914

NORTH AMERICA

UNITED STATES
DULLES Avery, S.I. ------------------------------- 24.08.1918
HICKEY James Aloysius -------------------------- 11.10.1920
BEVILACQUA Anthony Joseph ------------------- 17.06.1923
BAUM William Wakefield ------------------------- 21.11.1926
SZOKA Edmund Casimir ------------------------- 14.09.1927
MAIDA Adam Joseph ----------------------------- 18.03.1930
McCARRICK Theodore Edgar -------------------- 07.07.1930
KEELER William Henry --------------------------- 04.03.1931
LAW Bernard Francis ----------------------------- 04.11.1931
EGAN Edward Michael ---------------------------- 02.04.1932

STAFFORD James Francis ---------------------- 26.07.1932
MAHONY Roger Michael ------------------------ 27.02.1936
GEORGE Francis Eugene, O.M.I. -------------- 16.01.1937

CANADA
VACHON Louis-Albert ---------------------------- 04.02.1912
CARTER Gerald Emmett ------------------------- 01.03.1912
GAGNON Edouard, P.S.S. ---------------------- 15.01.1918
AMBROZIC Aloysius Matthew ------------------ 27.01.1930
TURCOTTE Jean-Claude------------------------- 26.06.1936

LATIN AMERICA
BRAZIL
de ARAÚJO SALES Eugênio -------------------- 08.11.1920
ARNS Paulo Evaristo, O.F.M.------------------- 14.09.1921
de ARAÚJO FERNANDES Serafim ----------- 13.08.1924
LORSCHEIDER Aloísio, O.F.M.----------------- 08.10.1924
NEVES MOREIRA Lucas, O.P. ----------------- 16.09.1925
FALCÃO FREIRE José ------------------------- 23.10.1925
AGNELO Geraldo Majella---------------------- 19.10.1933
HUMMES Cláudio, O.F.M. ---------------------- 08.08.1934

MEXICO
CORRIPIO AHUMADA Ernesto ---------------- 29.06.1919
SUÁREZ RIVERA Adolfo Antonio -------------- 09.01.1927
SANDOVAL ÍÑIGUEZ Juan------------------- 28.03.1933
RIVERA CARRERA Norberto ------------------- 06.06.1942

ARGENTINA
ARAMBURU Juan Carlos---------------------- 11.02.1912
PRIMATESTA Raúl Francisco ----------------- 14.04.1919
MEJÍA Jorge María ----------------------------- 31.01.1923
BERGOGLIO Jorge Mario, S.I. ----------------- 17.12.1936

COLOMBIA
CASTRILLÓN HOYOS Darío-------------------- 04.07.1929
RUBIANO SÁENZ Pedro ----------------------- 13.09.1932
LÓPEZ TRUJILLO Alfonso---------------------- 08.11.1935

CHILE
FRESNO LARRAÍN Juan Francisco------------- 26.07.1914
MEDINA ESTÉVEZ Jorge Arturo--------------- 23.12.1926
ERRÁZURIZ OSSA Francisco Javier----------- 05.09.1933

VENEZUELA
CASTILLO LARA Rosalio José, S.D.B. --------- 04.09.1922
VELASCO GARCÍA Ignacio Antonio, S.D.B. -- 17.01.1929

NICARAGUA
OBANDO BRAVO Miguel, S.D.B -------------- 02.02.1926

PUERTO RICO
APONTE MARTÍNEZ Luis----------------------- 04.08.1922

DOMINICAN REPUBLIC
LÓPEZ RODRÍGUEZ Nicolás de Jesús ------- 31.10.1936

CUBA
ORTEGA Y ALAMINO Jaime Lucas ----------- 18.10.1936

ECUADOR
GONZÁLEZ ZUMÁRRAGA Antonio José ------- 18.03.1925

HONDURAS
RODRÍGUEZ MARADIAGA Oscar Andrés, S.D.B.-- 29.12.1942

PERÙ
CIPRIANI THORNE Juan Luis----------------- 28.12.1943

BOLIVIA
TERRAZAS SANDOVAL Julio, C.SS.R.--------- 07.03.1936

AFRICA
NIGERIA
ARINZE Francis -------------------------------- 01.11.1932

ANGOLA
do NASCIMENTO Alexandre -------------------- 01.03.1925

BENIN
GANTIN Bernardin ----------------------------- 08.05.1922

CAMEROON
TUMI Christian Wiyghan ----------------------- 15.10.1930

ETHIOPIA
TZADUA Paulos ---------------------------------- 25.08.1921

KENYA
OTUNGA Maurice Michael ------------------------ --.01.1923

MOZAMBIQUE
SANTOS Alexandre José Maria dos, O.F.M.----- 18.03.1924

CONGO
ETSOU-NZABI-BAMUNGWABI Frédéric, C.I.C.M 03.12.1930

UGANDA
WAMALA Emmanuel ------------------------------ 15.12.1926

MADAGASCAR
RAZAFINDRATANDRA Armand Gaétan ---------- 07.08.1925

TANZANIA
PENGO Polycarp ---------------------------------- 05.08.1944

IVORY COAST
AGRÉ Bernard------------------------------------ 02.03.1926

SOUTH AFRICA
NAPIER Wilfrid Fox, O.F.M. ---------------------- 08.03.1941

SENEGAL
THIANDOUM Hyacinthe --------------------------- 02.02.1921

MAURITIUS
MARGÉOT Jean ----------------------------------- 03.02.1916

EGYPT
GHATTAS Stéphanos II, C.M. -------------------- 16.01.1920

ASIA
INDIA
PIMENTA Simon Ignatius ------------------------ 01.03.1920
LOURDUSAMY D. Simon--------------------------- 05.02.1924
VITHAYATHIL Varkey, C.SS.R. -------------------- 29.05.1927
DIAS Ivan--- 14.04.1936

PHILIPPINES
SÁNCHEZ José T.--------------------------------- 17.03.1920
SIN Jaime L. ------------------------------------- 31.08.1928
VIDAL Ricardo J. -------------------------------- 06.02.1931

VIETNAM
PHAM ĐÌNH TUNG Paul Joseph------------------- 15.06.1919
NGUYÊN VAN THUÂN François Xavier----------- 17.04.1928

CHINA
WU CHENG-CHUNG John Baptist --------------- 26.03.1925

TAIWAN
SHAN KUO-HSI Paul, S.I. ------------------------ 03.12.1923

JAPAN
SHIRAYANAGI Peter Seiichi----------------------- 17.06.1928

KOREA
KIM SOU-HWAN Stephen ------------------------- 08.05.1922

THAILAND
KITBUNCHU Michael Michai----------------------- 25.01.1929

INDONESIA
DARMAATMADJA Julius Riyadi, S.I. ------------- 20.12.1934

SYRIA
DAOUD Ignace Moussa I-------------------------- 18.09.1930

LEBANON
SFEIR Nasrallah Pierre -------------------------- 15.05.1920

OCEANIA
AUSTRALIA
CLANCY Edward Bede ---------------------------- 13.12.1923
CASSIDY Edward Idris---------------------------- 05.07.1924

SAMOA
TAOFINU'U Pio, S.M.------------------------------ 08.12.1923

NEW ZEALAND
WILLIAMS Thomas Stafford------------------------ 20.03.1930

LIST OF CARDINALS IN ALPHABETICAL ORDER

Printed in Italy May 2001
by Arti Grafiche Pomezia (Rome)